RECIPES
from an
ITALIAN
FARMHOUSE

RECIPES
from an
ITALIAN
FARMHOUSE

VALENTINA HARRIS

Special photography by
Linda Burgess

conran
OCTOPUS

For Diana with infinite thanks and fondest love

This edition published 1989 by
Conran Octopus Limited
2-4 Heron Quays
London E14 4JP
www.conran-octopus.co.uk

This paperback edition published
in 1993 by Conran Octopus Limited

Reprinted 1993, 1994, 1995, 1996, 1999

Project Editor – Lorraine Dickey
Editors – Pepita Aris, Scott Ewing
Art Director – Mary Evans
Designer – Christine Wood
Picture Research – Nadine Bazar
Production – Julia Golding
Photographic Stylist – Debbie Patterson
Painted tiles – Barbara Mullarney Wright
Line Artwork – Penny Lovelock
Editorial Assistant – Elizabeth Brooks

British Library Cataloguing in Publication Data
Harris, Valentina
Recipes from an Italian farmhouse
1. Food: Italian dishes. Recipes
I. Title
641.5945

ISBN 1 84091 149 2

Typeset by Elite Typesetting Techniques, Southampton
Printed and bound in China

CONTENTS

FOREWORD

Valentina harris has combined farmhouses from many of Italy's regions into one idealized farmhouse in which they cook rustic dishes from all over the peninsula. The Minestrone in this house may be from Lombardy, Liguria or Emilia-Romagna; the meat dishes may come from Sicily, Sienna or Abruzzi – they are at once traditional, and enlivened by a personal touch. Tuscan though I am, I had never come across a Florentine Castagnaccio made with carraway seeds, but I couldn't wait to try it once I saw this version.

Growing up in an Italian farmhouse or villa, as I did for part of my childhood, is surely the most ideal youthful existence imaginable, and one regrets that so few people today can know that experience. But going through Ms Harris's book brought it all back to me, as I'm sure it will evoke this life both for those who remember it and for many, many others for whom it is a dream. The cornmeal and rice cakes that we made for holidays, the hearty bean soups, the frittate – all are here.

When many still lived on farms in Italy, there was a vast repertory of recipes, some of which were made only seasonally, and others just once a year on a particular feast day. Now we have secularized these dishes and can enjoy them at any time, regardless of their traditional season. If we have lost some reverberations, we have gained in freedom: the freedom to enjoy a favorite Christmas or Easter dish at any time of the year, according to our whim. Many of the sweets in this book, too, are of the sort once associated only with a particular holiday; but here they are, and let us eat them as we like.

Italy has for a long time indulged in a kind of inverse snobbery as regards food. Country dishes, often called admiringly "la cucina povera" (that is, poor food), are eaten by members of the nobility, who in common with some characters in Proust, like to present themselves as "country people". In the cities too, in Florence, Venice, and Rome, one speaks glowingly of the "genuine" food of the country. Fortunately, inverse or not, this is not just snobbery – country food long ago passed the test of time and remains extraordinarily satisfying. Even those who appreciate the very sophisticated cooking, "alta cucina", and Italy has much of it, find a place for these rustic marvels. And while "alta cucina", arising out of court cooking, shares many similarities from region to region, vernacular cooking is as varied as the many dialects of a language.

Valentina Harris, in this special book which is both traditional in its base and also quite personal in some of its interpretations, gives us a warm and lively experience of this world of food which we must strive to preserve, because it is beginning to disappear, along with the way of life which gave it birth. This book will help to keep the spirit of it alive. Here we have soups, pastas, rice dishes, a wide variety of main courses: meat, fish, eggs, and an array of desserts. Together these recipes reflect the varied traditions of our great country and its "cucina".

Giuliano Bugialli

THE BASIC INGREDIENTS

THIS BOOK IS ABOUT ITALIAN COOKERY of the most rustic and uncomplicated sort. The recipes are for the most part classic and traditional family favorites with more than a hint of nostalgia. Italian cooking has its origins firmly embedded in Italy's history of poverty and peasant farming, and these are the dishes that rose directly out of such circumstances.

As a matter of course, I have adapted these very old recipes for use with modern appliances. Not many of us have the facilities that the originators of the dishes would have had, such as the embers of a real wood fire in which to leave the casserole on a slow cook for almost a night or a day. Although these dishes are born of the simplest life imaginable, it is a simplicity rich in the best that nature has to offer. If you observe the rules, and use the freshest herbs, good quality olive oil, and patient cooking, then you will taste the dishes in their true essence.

When vegetables are grown in small quantities, as is the practice on Italian farms, and with plenty of good old-fashioned organic manure, they have a flavor worlds removed from plastic-wrapped, mass-produced vegetables. National differences also have to be taken into account — some American tomatoes, for example, have nothing like the flavor of their Italian counterparts, and you may have to give them a little help with a dab of tomato paste. But this is all in the spirit of peasant cookery, which is anything but a precise art.

It is worth pointing out here that there is no such thing as a generic "Italian" cuisine: the cooking of my country is absolutely and obviously regional. What is enjoyed in snow-bound Friuli will quite literally be spat upon under the burning skies of arrogant Calabria. In the book I have included recipes from the length and breadth of the geographical "boot," including the islands, to give you some inkling of how different the dishes are depending upon where they originate. This is done in no particular order, so you will jump from north to south and east to west. But all the recipes illustrate the need for thrift and a flair for stretching the available ingredients, and this is exactly what made them popular in the first place.

Eating is a ritual in Italy, a very special moment when the family gathers together, where an extra place will always be set for the unexpected visitor. This is not food for making an impression, it is everyday *real* food which can be managed by almost anybody. I have no time for fussy cooking which pretends to the exactness of a chemical equation — for me cooking is essentially intuitive. With a little care and love, I like to cook the food which evolved out of necessity, availability and hunger — but which tastes as good now as it did then, food which will feed your body and soul and won't make a bottomless hole in your wallet. Perhaps it is time to adapt our cooking habits slightly, and choose foods that are as simple and humble as the fields and the sea. For all these reasons, I am delighted to be able to bring you this very much loved side of the cooking of my Italy.

BUON APPETITO!

Valentina Harris

CHEESE

Cheese has been a basic dish on the poorest tables for centuries. Italy boasts more varieties of cheese than even France, much of it still craft-made — the flavor reflecting its place of origin. Many excellent cheeses are exported and are easily obtainable in delicatessens and supermarkets.

PARMESAN

Parmigiano reggiano, made in Emiglia Romagna, is the most famous of the grana cheeses, which mature to be very grainy and hard and are therefore used for grating. Grana padano is a very similar cheese made in Lombardy, with its name stamped repeatedly over the hard rind.

Parmesan is one of Italy's oldest cheeses. It's also the biggest and aged the longest time. It is made from skimmed cows' milk in a big wheel — the whole cheese weighing at least 52 lb. As a general rule, the older the cheese, the more expensive it will be. Parmigiano stravecchio is aged a minimum of 2 years. Parmesan is so hard that a wedge-shaped knife is used to split rather than cut the cheese, leaving untidy rough-hewn lumps. Buy these rather than already-grated cheese, which lacks the slightly pineapple taste of the real thing.

Young Parmesan is delicious eaten in hunks with raw young vegetables, but it is most famous as a condiment. It should be sprinkled over the dish after cooking, rather than included in a sauce. A good Parmesan has a granular, even texture.

PECORINO

Pecorino is a pungent sheeps' milk cheese produced in every province of the center and south. It matures more quickly than Parmesan — becoming hard in about 8 months — so in Italy it is the cheaper cheese. It is used for grating and cooking.

Pecorino romano is well-liked for its pepper flavor, while the Sardinian pecorino sardo is slightly sharp. These cheeses weigh 3–8 lb and have a distinctive shape, bulging out halfway down the side: the Italians call this "humpback." The inside is always dense and straw-colored, while the rind is a guide to age — yellowish when young though turns to a reddish-black for the older cheeses.

PROVOLONE AND CACIOCAVALLO

A familiar cheese from southern Italy, provolone comes in many fanciful shapes, often indented by the strings that contain it. The large oval, from which it derives its name, is the most common form.

It is a pasta filata cheese, which means that the curds are stretched out in long strips, then bundled together in layers. It should be white or pale straw-colored and it may develop moist holes when mature. Three main kinds are produced: mild (dolce), sharp (piccante), and smoked (affumicato).

Made in much the same way, caciocavallo are linked in pairs like saddlebags, which explains their Italian name ("a cavallo" means "on horseback"). They are kneaded in warm water and are traditionally shaped by hand.

STRACCHINO

Stracchino is a generic name for the summer cheeses, a group of cows' milk cheeses made in northern Italy (particularly Lombardy and Piedmont). Made from milk which is considerably thinner, the cheeses are semi-soft and delicate, maturing quickly.

Crescenza is rindless and the softer version is slightly wet, sold wrapped in paper. Gorgonzola is a crescenza which has blued and matured, and so can be used for melting on food or coated with bread crumbs and fried.

The square Taleggio is the best known as one of the oldest soft cheeses. It has a soft, rosy rind and the taste is more mature than crescenza.

MOZZARELLA

Mozzarella is a native of Campania, where water buffaloes were introduced in the 16th century. Buffalo milk cheeses are still exported, but are becoming increasingly rare, even in Italy, and those made with cows' milk are the norm. Mozzarella is a fresh wet cheese, low in fat, sold packed in its own whey, which may be part of the weight given on the package. It is a pasta filata cheese, made from long strips of curd, cut and wrapped in little bundles — mozzata means cut. Standard sizes are: 4–5 oz and 7–9 oz.

Mozzarella is forever associated with pizza — and beloved by Italians — because of the way it binds other ingredients together when it melts.

RICOTTA

A soft, creamy-looking, fresh ewes' milk cheese, made from whey, low in fat, ricotta is identifiable by the mark of the basket in which it is drained. It has a crumbly texture and a curiously rich, but bland flavor which is brought out by cooking.

It is a favorite for pasta stuffings and also for cheesecakes. Half-and-half cream cheese and cottage cheese makes a passable substitute.

SALUMI

Salumi means preserved meat — the equivalent of the French charcuterie — all those pork products that are eaten sliced. There are almost as many ways of preserving pork in Italy as there are cheeses. Most of them, like the bacons and salami, keep well. But a few, like Coppa Senese, for which I have given a recipe, and cotechino, described below, though preserved meat, should nevertheless be eaten within 3 days and kept in a cool place.

HAM

Ham is prosciutto and although Italy does produce cooked ham, called prosciutto cotto, raw ham is so famous that the word by itself means raw ham. Prosciutto is cured by salting and then air-dried. For eating immediately it is carved into the thinnest possible slices, though for cooking it may be cubed.

Parma ham — possibly the world's most famous ham — is the best-known prosciutto crudo and is slightly sweet. San Daniele ham is less sweet and also leaner. The curing process is a long one, the meat of the best quality, and so it is always expensive, particularly from the bone.

BACON

Pancetta is the salted, raw belly of pork, exactly the same cut as bacon. Pancetta arrotolata is commonest abroad, shaped like a long sausage, with the fat belly wrapped around the lean back meat. Some pancetta is smoked — affumicata. Pancetta is the basis of many Italian dishes, cubes being fried with onions and probably other vegetables and herbs, until the onion softens. It's used so often that this "soffritto" is often just listed as an ingredient in Italian recipe books.

Fatty bacon, or cubed fat cut from ham, can be substituted (though bacon sometimes contains water, which pancetta never does).

Guanciale is a specialty from Latium around Rome. It is the pig's cheek — the same cut as pig's jowl. The meat is salted and cured like bacon, and bacon is the usual substitute.

SALAMI

These preserved sausages are made all over the country and in innumerable different, local forms. The firm, pinkish-red ones, flecked with white fat are a familiar sight, but in some parts of Italy the salami meat is soft and is kept in jars covered with lard. Firm salami keep well hanging up, but they should be eaten once cut.

Bologna's famous mortadella is much copied and is said to take its name from the mortar in which the meat was ground. The pink lean pork is finely ground, flavored with peppercorns and garlic, and then dotted with the white of lard strips, which run down the sausage. Big mortadelle can be as much as 16 inches across and proportionately as long.

Salame milano is probably the most popular sausage outside Italy. The texture is fine and some include beef as well as pork. As a general rule, the further south you go, the more highly seasoned the salami — salami di Napoli include chilies. Cacciatore are a rather hard small, salami bought whole. Another huge one is finocchiona, whose name refers to the wild fennel with which it is flavored.

In Italy look for casalingo, which are the farm-made salami; they are usually coarser than mass-produced ones. A few are sold abroad under their regional names.

COTECHINO

Cotechino is a preserved meat which nevertheless should be cooked soon after purchase. It contains lean meat from the head and neck of the pig, well-spiced, but the most important ingredient is chopped, salted pork rind. With slow cooking this fat becomes jellied and oozes out when the sausage is cut. For this reason it is always served with lentils, boiled potatoes, or beans to soak up the fat.

To cook, prick it in several places with a fork, wrap in a cloth and boil for 2–3 hours. Cotechino cotto is precooked and sold as boil-in-the-bag. This keeps very well for long periods, then only takes 20 minutes to cook.

COOKING FATS

Butter used to be confined to Lombardy, near the French border. Traditionally the basic cooking fat comes from beneath the pig's skin, particularly in provinces without olive trees.

It is sold as salted pork fat, lardo, which keeps well, or melted down called strutto. Now, in these cholesterol-conscious days there is a shift to olive oil and sunflower seed oil.

Olive oil is the base of southern farmhouse cookery. It is also relatively low in cholesterol. It has its home in the south, and becomes richer and stronger the further south you go.

There are four grades of olive oil: second pressing oil is not worth bothering about — it was once used for lighting the street-lamps! A pure, virgin olive oil is exactly what it says it is — and will be sufficient for the recipes in this book.

A greenish, strong, fruity extra vergine is best suited for salads. Superfino oil is the top class and retails at wine prices — make it a special treat for feast days!

STARCHES

Italians are accustomed to getting their carbohydrates in much more varied ways than just the choices of potatoes and bread eaten further north.

PASTA

Pasta comes in an infinite variety of forms, but its ingredients are utterly simple — flour and water — sometimes with added oil. Dried pasta is made from durum wheat — the hardest sort — and consequently is more nutritious. Only one traditional pasta — bigoli — is made with whole-wheat. Homemade pasta is always made with plain flour, because it is easier to roll this very thinly. Eggs are sometimes added to give richness, when it becomes pasta all 'uovo. The old peasant rule was a 1 egg quantity per person — too much for us now!

In many Italian towns and now in Italian delicatessens abroad, they make and sell fresh pasta on a daily basis. However, once you acquire the knack, it is not difficult to make at home. All the pasta recipes in this book tell you how to make your own pasta — because it is the traditional way, and also because it is light and delicious (but most of the pasta recipes in this book can be made with dried pasta if necessary).

Despite its association with Italy as a whole, pasta is the staple of the south of Italy, where it has been the food of the poor for more than two centuries.

The secret of cooking pasta is to use large quantities of boiling water. Drain and serve it the moment it is tender — still with a little bite. There are three main ways of serving it. In past 'asciutta a plain pasta is dressed with a sauce. A pasta in brodo is a fine plain pasta or a delicately stuffed pocket, cooked for a few minutes in broth. Pasta al forno ("in the oven") is baked in layers in a sauce.

COUSCOUS

Cuscusa was an Arab introduction to Italy long ago. Like pasta it is made from durum wheat. Sicilian peasants make it in the classic way, by rolling together two varieties of semolina. You can also buy North African dried couscous, which must be steamed for the same time. Easiest of all is the instant couscous: 1lb 2 oz needs soaking in $2\frac{1}{2}$ cups boiling water for 10 minutes. Then it should be set over a low heat and fresh broth poured in, stirring all the while.

RICE

What pasta is to the south, rice is to northern Italian cooking. It was introduced by the Saracens and has been cultivated in Lombardy since the 14th century. Spanish rulers then introduced paella and from this evolved Italy's most famous rice dish, risotto.

For risotto, there is really no substitute for the large, round-grained rices which are grown in Piedmont, Lombardy, and the Veneto.

There are four grades of Italian rice, but fino and superfino are best for risotto, because they keep their shape and firmness during slow cooking. Arborio superfino is sold outside Italy, but vialone, roma and carnaroli are difficult to find. Round grain, ordinario, rice is best for sweets.

American long-grain rices can be used for risotto, but the results will not be the same because they are pre-washed to keep the grains separate after cooking. In a risotto regular stirring encourages the rice to become starchy and bind together.

POLENTA

Polenta is the Italian name for both the flour that we know as cornmeal and the dish made from it. Dried maize is ground into meal which may be either coarse, medium or fine. It may also be yellow or white — the latter is preferred for fish. For three hundred years it has been the staff of life in much of Lombardy and all of northern Venetia.

To make polenta, the cornmeal is trickled into boiling salted water and stirred over low heat, until a thick porridge is formed. The amount of water is given on the package and varies by brand, but usually 1 lb absorbs $7\frac{1}{2}$ cups. This takes $30-40$ minutes according to brand — cheaper polentas, sold loose, take longer. The polenta is ready when it clings to the spoon and comes away from the side of the pan. In northern Italy traditionally a special pan is kept for it, a copper paiuolo, without a tin lining.

The polenta can be served just as it is, or it may be left to set and then cut into slices. These can then be baked like lasagne, or are commonly fried to serve as an accompaniment. It can also be made into flat cakes.

BREAD

Many Italian recipes use bread as a base. Soups are poured over bread, slices and crumbs are used for stuffing, and a delicious dolce is made from leftover bread and candied fruit.

Crostini are toasts for topping, while bruschetta is served as an accompaniment. Made of slices of coarse white bread baked in the oven until crisp and golden — or on a charcoal grill — they are rubbed with garlic then anointed with a little olive oil. Pizza, which is simply bread dough baked with a flavorful sauce, is the pride of the south.

LEGUMES AND GRAINS

Legumes and all sorts of other dried vegetables are the staples of the winter kitchen in poor communities.

BEANS

For centuries, fagioli or dried beans have provided farmers with a good source of protein. Fresh beans have vitamins as well and are preferred for their taste but dried provide security for the winter.

Traditionally, beans were soaked overnight with baking soda to soften the skins. Nowadays it is considered preferable to cover the beans with boiling water and soak for a hour.

Dried beans are always brought to a boil and boiled hard for a few minutes before simmering, because it has been discovered that red beans, in particular, contain a harmful enzyme that is not killed by simmering at low temperatures. One to 1½ hours is needed for modern strains of dried beans which cook somewhat faster than older varieties. Salt is not supposed to be added until the end, because it hardens the beans. Nowadays soup will probably contain 2 oz beans per person, with other vegetables: for a peasant dish this would be doubled.

The best-known type of kidney bean is borlotti; it's always speckled red, on a background that can be anything from pink to dark red. These are frequently cooked with a ham bone or some pork belly.

The handsome white cannellini beans (shown on page 32) are a Tuscan specialty. They can be small or large but are always elongated — green beans can be substituted. In general, different varieties of kidney beans are interchangeable in recipes.

Because of their tough skins, though, dried broad (fava) beans are an exception to this rule. These beans are an important food in the poorer south of Italy.

CHICK PEAS

Ceci are used in Italy in thick soups and even for a pasta sauce. They are often cooked with pork fat in some form, because their mealy texture provides the perfect foil. One of the oldest examples is Ceci con la zampina di maiale (page 70).

Soak chick peas like legumes. Cooking times can vary quite widely by brand, from 30 minutes to more than an hour. Surprisingly the larger ones cook fastest, because these come from improved modern strains.

CORN

Introduced in the 17th century, maize is known as granturco, "turkish corn." Ground to polenta, it became a staple, while dried maize was also stewed.

Nowadays, dried maize is either chicken feed or made into popcorn. The latter is useless for stewing in traditional recipes because it has an extremely hard outer skin, designed to hold it together until it explodes, so I have substituted kernels of fresh corn.

NUTS

The walnut, noce, grows throughout the country, though it is cooked mainly in the north. The old-style walnut sauces, often with bread, are now used mainly as stuffings.

Almonds, mandorle, make stuffings and are ground for thickening sauces and soups. But the use of almonds for dolce — often very sweet — is an Eastern Mediterranean legacy.

CHESTNUTS

Chestnuts, castagne, used to be a staple food in the north of Italy, where they still appear in several cooked dishes. They were also dried and ground to make flour and a predecessor of polenta. Nowadays, chestnut flour is used for cakes like Castagnaccio. Better Italian delicatessens stock it in winter and spring, for it has a short shelf life. It can be made by grinding dried nuts, then sifting the results.

PINE NUTS

Pine nuts, pinoli, or pignoli, are extracted from the huge cones of the umbrella pine. These slender cream-colored little nuts have a unique flavor, slightly aromatic, at once astringent and rich.

SPICES

Apart from fresh lemon, always on the tree outside her door, the farmer's wife often uses the following:

JUNIPER BERRIES

Juniper berries, ginepro, are little blue-black fruits with an aromatic-bitter taste, related to pine. Italian juniper is far stronger than that found further north and flavors meat and liqueurs.

CINNAMON

Rolled cinnamon bark, or cannella, can be ground to a powder at home. In Italy it is used for meat and game as well as the more usual sweet dishes.

MEAT, POULTRY AND GAME

Poorer households make do without much fresh meat. The highlight of the year is the autumn pig slaughter, which gives fresh maiale (pork) briefly, and a series of salumi for storing. Spicy fresh sausages, salsicce, are common.

Manzo, beef, is eaten more in the north of the country than the south. The stewing cuts of both beef and veal may end up in a big pot cooking slowly in the embers. Better cuts are used economically, for example, in a sauce.

Lambs are often killed at the beginning of summer and I have included several shepherds' recipes for lamb, some using the expensive cuts.

ORGAN MEATS

Please, please don't skip this. There is a tendency to regard variety meats as a food which the poor ate out of necessity — they did — that can now be discarded. This is not so. Many innards and extremities have special qualities or textures which make them kitchen delicacies still. The traditional recipe for calf's head, for instance pays for the effort it takes to find the meat.

Italy is proud of its fegato, liver dishes. Tuscany is known for both pigs' liver and its chicken livers, which are very large. But best of all is calves' liver which has an exquisite texture.

Sweetbreads, animelle, are less well known, but prized for their perfect white and delicate texture. Each animal has two, one from the throat and one nearer the heart and they are usually sold as a set. Peel off the membrane, soak for three hours in cold water, then blanch them.

Tripe, trippa, is the animal's stomach lining. As cows, in particular, have several stomachs, the tripes vary; the best is known as honeycomb tripe.

Buy calves' tripe if you can, but you may well find that the only tripe on sale is from a much older animal. This needs blanching and scraping, and far longer cooking. However, it is invariably sold dressed, that is, prepared and three-quarters cooked. It can then be finished following the recipe for a younger animal.

Pigs' feet, zampone, were prized for the way that long cooking turns the rind into a meat jelly. They are traditionally cooked with legumes or chick peas to soak up the juices.

CHICKEN

Pollo, the barnyard fowl, scratched for her living or ate the same dried maize that fed the poor farmer's family. Buy a free-range or corn-fed (maize-fed) chicken. The latter are yellow in color and so are easy to spot.

GAME

Wild rabbits, coniglio, caught after feeding on the erbe odorose, wild herbs, taste much better than our tame bunnies — their white meat is very good. Hare, lepre, is popular in northern Italy and Tuscany, but my recipe is from the south.

The Italians have always been fanatic hunters, as the clattering of gunshot in season will testify. Pheasant, duck and songbirds all go down. My recipe for pigeon on the spit represents a tradition of game barbecued outdoors.

I have not included any recipes for boar because it is hard to get hold of, but it deserves a mention. There are lots of them in the forests around Lucca. They have the gamiest of all game flavors — and are extremely chewy.

FISH

Italy's long coastline means she is well supplied with sea fish while lake and river fish appear in local recipes. Cooking methods are simple, like marinating, then grilling or baking. Generally Italians cook the fish with the head and tail, to keep the flavor, though a big fish like turbot will not be cooked in one piece. There are also some wonderful fish soups.

PIKE

Pike, luccio, are caught in the mountains of the north and center. This taper-shaped predator with its ugly mouth is a mass of little bones embedded in flesh. For this reason the more sophisticated recipes will serve pike boned and puréed. My recipe is an old one — the luccio is served whole, leaving the eater with the choice of extracting the bones or chewing them! You might prefer a solid piece of boneless monkfish or tuna.

RED AND GRAY MULLET

The red mullet, triglia, is the most highly-prized fish of the Mediterranean. Apart from its beautiful color, it can be cooked whole without cleaning. Sizes vary from 6–15 in. Scrape off the sequin-like scales by drawing a knife from the tail towards the head.

The gray mullet is called cefalo or muggine. It has a distinctive torpedo-shaped body, with a black back and needs careful cleaning if it was not taken from clean water.

DORADE

The dorade (or porgy) is a large fish with silvery scales, somewhat similar in taste to the sea bream.

RASCASSE

The scorfano or scorpion fish is chiefly famous as the fish for broth.

SARDINES

Pilchards – and many other little fish – go under the name of sarde. These stubby little silver fish, with a blue-green sheen and large papery scales swim in shoals off the south coast and are commonly served grilled.

EEL

The common eel spends a large part of its life in fresh water and the best come from the lagoon at Comacchio on the east coast. Other eels are fished from the sea and there are many ways of cooking them. The anguilla looks somewhat primitive, but the whitish flesh is delicious roasted or stewed.

Allow for the weight of the head and bony tail when purchasing. Fresh water eels have fat under the skin at certain times of year, so must be skinned. Tie a string around the head under the gills and attach this to a fixed point. Then nick the skin at the back of the head, get a grip with salted fingers and pull – like pulling off an adhesive strip. Alternatively, get your fish market to do it!

ANCHOVY

Anchovies are called acciuga in the north of Italy, and alice around Naples. It is impossible to confuse fresh anchovies with sardines because they are very slender with a sharp nose. Their sides are silvery and the blue-green back turns dark blue or black as more time out of the water elapses. They are best appreciated raw in a vinaigrette marinade.

There are two ways of preserving them; in oil and by layering them with salt in small barrels – better Italian delicatessens abroad stock these. Prepare barrel anchovies by washing them, then splitting them open to remove the bones from the inside. In Italy anchovies are used as a flavoring ingredient for beans and stews.

DRIED FISH

Dried cod is one of the staples of the Italian peasant. There are two different ways of curing it and recipes for either can be used interchangeably, provided the fish is soaked first for the appropriate amount of time.

Stoccafisso, stockfish, has been eaten by Italian peasants for 500 years, because it is dried hard and so is absolutely safe in summer temperatures. It is not salted, but is wind-dried, gutted, and the head removed, but is otherwise fish-shaped.

Baccalà (confusingly, the Venetians use this term for stoccafisso): are beheaded, split open, and salted on the ship, then dried on land. They are like thick, triangular cardboard sheets, salty and smelling faintly, and can be a considerable size. Of the two baccalà are much easier to find in any Mediterranean delicatessen.

Stockfish needs to be beaten to break the fibers, and then soaked – usually for 3 days. Salt cod needs 24 hours soaking – done in a bowl in a sink under a running tap to avoid any smell. Judge the soaking time by the rest of the recipe. Thick pieces from the center of the fish are often fried, thinner trimmings flavor stews with tomatoes and other vegetables. The fish must be very moist if there is no further stewing. Lucky Italians can buy these fish already-prepared!

SHELLFISH

The main rule for clams and mussels is to discard open ones before you start and closed ones after cooking

SQUID AND OCTOPUS

The torpedo-shaped squid, with two fins at the end opposite the tentacles are called calamari. Cuttlefish, seppie, are flatter with a frilly fin all around and two of the tentacles are much longer. Big ones may be stuffed, others cut into strips and fried, and tiny ones served whole.

The preparation is very similar. Pull up the tentacles to turn out the contents of the sac (being careful not to puncture the ink bag, which is kept in some recipes). Cut off the tentacles above the eyes and discard everything else. Flex the body slightly to dislodge the transparent cartilage of a squid. Large cuttlefish must be slit down the side to remove the white cuttle bone. Rub off the dark skin with salted hands.

Remove the eyes and beak of an octopus, pulpo, and clean inside. For bigger ones you will need to make a slit up to the head and peel the skin off the tentacles, with the rings in the suckers. After this give them a good thumping, like tenderizing a steak.

SCAMPI

The head and claws of the larger scampi have edible insides. The back shell is firmer than a shrimp's, with spiky edges, and the stomach is protected. To snap the stomach shell, squeeze the two sides together, then peel the legs up and over the back – like taking off a saddle. Pinch the tail fin with one hand to release suction and pull the whole body out with the other hand.

VEGETABLES

The delights of the Italian vegetable garden are basic to Italian cooking. Vegetables which are well known elsewhere have special uses in Italian dishes. For example, celery and carrots are a standard soup flavoring and are frequently part of soffrito (see Bacon).

Some vegetables are particularly identified with the south; eggplant, melanzana, has been eaten there for 900 years. It's important to remove the bitter juices by salting, washing, and draining. It will otherwise absorb huge amounts of oil during cooking.

Peppers, peperoni, which give such color, grow to a huge size in the south, where they are grilled or stuffed. The related chili, peperoncini, is also an identifiably southern flavoring.

CHARD AND BITTER LEAVES

Coste, often known as Swiss chard, is popular around the Mediterranean and becoming better known elsewhere. Fashion has gone in a complete circle and now it is grown for the thick stems, which have a flavor faintly reminiscent of asparagus, rather than the fleshy dark leaves, which have been used for so long. Chard combines well with pine nuts.

Spinach, spinaci, is not a long-established Italian vegetable, but it has been enthusiastically embraced, and can be substituted for chard, as can the leafy tops of beets and turnips.

CHICORY AND ENDIVE

The small white torpedo-shaped plant called Belgian endive in the United States and chicory in Britain does not appear in traditional Italian cooking, but its leafier cousins do. Red radicchio

is part of the family, as is wild chicory, a traditional peasant food more bitter to the taste. Curly endive is nearer to the wild salad; it can be soaked briefly before use to get rid of some of the bitterness.

ARUGULA

Arugula is a peppery salad vegetable. It is a common ingredient in salad leaf mixtures in Italian markets, added to other leaves to make them more interesting. Usually several varieties are on sale. Young spinach is more bitter and less sharp but will do as a substitute.

ZUCCHINI AND THEIR FLOWERS

These tiny marrows, less than 6 in long, though they can grow much larger, can be green or yellow and are very popular in Italy. Their Italian name, zucchini, traveled with them to America, although the British use the French name, courgettes.

The orange flowers are a delicacy deep-fried or in omelets. They also look very attractive and are very popular with many chefs outside Italy. Soak them in water with lemon juice for 30 minutes before dehulling.

GLOBE ARTICHOKE

Italians delight in beautiful forms and the handsome carciofi are the huge buds of a type of thistle. They flourish in the limestone soils of south Italy, where they grow at great speed, which gives them excellent flavor. There are two main types, one with a pointed head and prickly leaves and one with a rounded head and no prickles.

In the south they are not eaten leaf by leaf as they are further north. Everything served can always be

eaten, so the chokes are always cleaned first and the tougher leaves removed. Small ones, with soft chokes, are cooked whole, and the hearts of larger ones are removed and served in other dishes. The texture and taste of Jerusalem artichokes makes them an acceptable substitute for most recipes.

FENNEL

The most Italian of vegetables, finocchio is sometimes called Florence fennel outside Italy, to distinguish it from the herb of the same name. Its overlapping stems look almost like a bulb and its feathery green tops are saved and used like an herb, for sprinkling. The sweetness of the vegetable is demonstrated by the old Italian custom of putting fennel on the table, like a fruit, at the end of a meal. It is equally good raw in salads, or cooked.

CELERIAC

In Italy this is called sedano rapa, which means a grating celery, and the root is similar in taste to celery, though it is not really a traditional Italian vegetable. The sweet flavor is strongest in the young roots weighing under 1 lb. Prepare it like a turnip, which can be used as a substitute. (Of the two, turnip has a tougher skin with more waste.) Keep the leaves of celeriac, if you can get them — they make a lovely additional seasoning.

SCORZONERA

This thin black root, like a carrot but twice as long, belongs to the dandelion family. The Italian name is used worldwide, since it was bred in Italy. Salsify is very similar to it, though unrelated, and can be used as a substitute.

The flavor is sweet and some say

oyster-like. To prepare it, remove the base of the roots and leafy tops, brush off the soil, and peel or scrape off the skin. It is then cut into 2−4 inches lengths. Keep it in some water made acidic with a little lemon juice until ready to cook; it is cooked when slightly softened.

ONIONS AND GARLIC

Indispensable as a flavoring for other vegetables, the cipolla is also eaten in its own right: roasted, stuffed, and in salads. There are several different varieties serving different purposes, the mildest coming from Piedmont. Red ones are used for salads and for their color in dishes like Fitascetta.

It would be impossible to imagine the Italian kitchen without aglio, garlic. Garlic is frequently fried first in cooking oil to flavor it. Together with onion it makes a basic kitchen preparation − battuto. Very finely chopped (the word means finely chopped), they are sautéed together in pork fat and this is the beginning of many, many country dishes.

TOMATOES

The pomodoro, or "golden apple" has been at the center of southern Italian cooking since the 18th century: Naples invented tomato sauce.

Really ripe tomatoes have few seeds and the skin peels off easily. A few seconds in boiling water may be necessary for less perfect northern specimens. In Italy plum tomatoes are invariably used for cooking, round ones are preferred for salads.

For more than a hundred years the south has canned tomatoes for export. A more recent export, now widely available, is the processed version, passata. The name means sieved, and it

is nothing more than natural-strength pulped tomato, conveniently without skin or seeds.

PORCINI

Ceps, porcini in Italy, are the best-flavored mushrooms of the boletus family. The cap of the fresh mushroom looks like a brown sugar-glazed bun, with a fat stalk. Dried, they are sold in all Italian delicatessens.

The flavor of the mushroom is enhanced and intensified by drying, so although it is quite expensive, 1 oz is usually enough for a dish. Soak dried porcini for about 20 minutes in warm water, then drain and slice. Add them towards the end of cooking time, so that they do not lose their flavor.

TRUFFLES

Tartufi are the kings of the edible fungi. Italy has two of the very best. The black truffle grows most profusely around Norcia and Spoleto in Umbria, where pigs are still trained to identify where they are hidden underground. They are in season, from October to December, and are the same truffle that is found in Périgord in France. A black truffle looks somewhat like a dirty potato. Cooking brings out its flavor. The so called white truffle − in reality a beige-brown − comes from around the town of Alba. The finest in the world, it is shaved raw over hot food.

Black truffles are sold vacuum-packed with a little liquid in jars, while even the peelings are canned. Once a wild food, available to all finders, the smell of truffle is so pervasive that it affects all food it contacts − hence, the rush to make truffle or truffle-and-mushroom pastes. Even truffle-flavored oil will give you a little taste of these luxuries.

HERBS

Some familiar herbs are used daily in Italian dishes: thyme with everything, rosemary for roasts and barbecues, wild fennel for fish and sausages, the bay leaf as a partner for fish and meat, and sage as almost obligatory in the north for pork and beans. Mint is used in imaginative combinations, while flat-leafed (Italian) parsley has more flavor than the curly one. Here are others, traditionally inseparable from Italian cooking.

OREGANO

Luckily for everyone, this is one of the few herbs that taste better dried. Drying accentuates its flavor. Oregano from the south is most pungent and is partnered with a wide range of foods.

BASIL

A sun-lover, basilico is the perfect partner for tomatoes. But in Liguria it is cultivated for pesto sauce, combined with Parmesan and pine nuts.

PREBOGGION

A mixed handful of wild herbs, sold in the markets of Genoa and gathered nearby, combine for one mass of flavor. Picking a bunch of wild herbs with as many varieties as possible is a common practice which need not be limited to Italy. Preboggion are used to flavor salads and stuffings alike.

CAPERS

Capers, capperi, are the tight buds of a Mediterranean shrub. They are preserved in sea salt and often in wine vinegar. They have a sharp taste and provide a good foil to olive oil and rich meats and sauces.

SOUPS

*There are few things more wholesome and
nutritious than a big bowl of real Italian
soup — perfect for cold winter evenings, rich
enough for a main meal in summertime.*

JOTA *left (p 31)*
MINESTRONE CON LA ZUCCA *right (p 21)*

THERE ARE FEW THINGS MORE WHOLESOME and nutritious than a big bowl of real, honest soup. In terms of the peasant household, where wasting food was rightly considered a cardinal sin, a soup neatly solved the problem of how to make something delicious out of leftovers. Minestrone translates literally as "Big Soup," in other words a soup which is an entire meal. It originated in Lombardy, a flat, uninterrupted landscape whose inhabitants are often fog- and snow-bound — making it a perfect setting for the eating of soup. Lombard farms tend to be enormous buildings with plenty of space for families and animals, fortresses against the inclement weather and unsympathetic intruders. Imagine, if you can, being trapped inside your vast farm in mid-winter. There is a huge fire roaring in the grate, and outside all is gray, dark, and damp. This is most certainly not the moment for a cheese soufflé with prawn sauce: what you need is a bowl filled with vegetables and rice or pasta, all simmered in the best-quality stock. Into the stock itself go any scrap leftovers — to be instantly transformed into something memorable!

In the recipes which come from further south you will discover a certain difference: although the soups are still nutritious and filling, they are considerably less rich and a great deal lighter. This is due principally to the difference in climate — the temperature of a Calabrian winter is somewhat milder than the winter in Friuli, unless you venture high up in the mountains, and even then you won't have the Alpine conditions of the northern areas. In the south, chili peppers are very popular for keeping you warm — an innocent-looking vegetable soup eaten in the Abruzzi villages could have you reaching for the water jug before you can swallow!

The soup recipes which use bread (as opposed to rice, beans, and legumes, pasta or potatoes) as their starch base do so purely for reasons of economy, and when you read them they may sound a bit tasteless. But the quality of the bread is the key — bread which is full of flavor and texture will be an admirable base for anything. When making these soups, try to get hold of bread which tastes like bread ought to taste — the homemade variety being the very best.

Tortellini in brodo — tortellini in a broth — is a very delicate and sophisticated way of serving pasta. The broth should be of the best quality, and it is most important that you seal the little pasta parcels very securely before boiling — if you don't they will almost certainly part company with their filling during cooking! They should be plunged into the broth for literally the very last minutes. It is customary to offer a garnish of grated Parmesan or pecorino cheese when serving soup, and also a little jug of olive oil to dribble over the soup before eating — this enhances the flavor and helps to cool the soup down.

As with all the recipes in this book, I very much hope that these soups will become close friends of yours, and therefore you must feel free to vary the recipes as you use them. After all, in their original settings they would have altered a great deal from one household to another depending on the availability of ingredients and that great unquantifiable, personal taste.

MINESTRONE ALLA LOMBARDA

LOMBARD MINESTRONE

This is the original 'big soup' – so stiff it is almost solid cold – containing lots of fresh vegetables, rice, and Parmesan cheese to nourish and satisfy.

SERVES 6

2 sticks celery, very finely chopped
2 carrots, scraped and very finely chopped
2 zucchini, finely sliced
3 medium-sized potatoes, peeled and left whole
1 lb ripe tomatoes
3 tablespoons pork drippings
a handful of fresh parsley leaves, washed and very finely chopped
1 large clove garlic, peeled and very finely chopped
1 large red onion, finely chopped
2 leaves fresh sage
5 slices of bacon, finely chopped
8 fresh basil leaves
1 cup fresh borlotti or pinto beans (or 4 oz dried – soaked overnight and brought back to a boil twice)
2 cups (8 oz) shelled green peas (frozen only if you really have no alternative)
¼ cabbage, coarsely chopped
½ teaspoon tomato paste
1 cup rice or small-sized, dried pasta
salt and pepper
freshly grated Parmesan cheese
olive oil

Prepare and mix the celery, carrots, zucchini, and potatoes. Dip the tomatoes in boiling water. Scoop them out with a slotted spoon, quickly peel, then chop them, discarding the seeds.

Put the drippings, parsley, and garlic in a 4 quart soup pot and mix well. Add the chopped onion, sage leaves, and bacon. Fry together very carefully until the onion is mushy and transparent, then add all the prepared vegetables, the basil, beans, and tomato paste.

Pour in 3 quarts cold water, cover and simmer for 3 hours, stirring occasionally. If at the end of this time the potatoes have not disintegrated into tiny bits, mash them in with a fork to thicken the soup.

If using fresh shelled peas, add them to the soup. After 15 minutes, add the cabbage leaves. Simmer for 15 minutes, then add the rice or pasta, with the frozen peas, if using. Cook rice for 20 minutes or pasta according to the manufacturer's instructions. Stir and taste and adjust the seasoning.

Serve hot in the winter time with olive oil to drizzle over the surface and Parmesan cheese in a bowl to sprinkle on to taste. In the summertime the soup is eaten cold, but not chilled. If wished, let the soup set in individual bowls overnight, then turn it out onto plates, but always serve it with olive oil and Parmesan cheese.

MINESTRONE CON LA ZUCCA

MINESTRONE WITH PUMPKIN

This soup always makes a good impression, it's so bright and warming and really does taste as good as it looks! Serve it with a fairly smooth white wine, such as an Italian Pinot, which is a good all round soup wine. It is also an excellent accompaniment to egg and cheese dishes and lake or river fish.

SERVES 4

2 lb yellow pumpkin, peeled, and seeded
salt and pepper
2½ cups good stock
2 cups milk
2 oz spaghetti, broken into small pieces
2 tablespoons unsalted butter
¾ cup freshly grated Parmesan cheese

Cut the pumpkin into chunks. Bring a large saucepan of salted water to a boil, add the pumpkin, and cook until tender. Drain and mash to a puree. Return to the pan, pour in the stock and milk, and stir.

Bring back to a boil, stir in the pasta, and cook until tender. Taste and season. Remove the pan from the heat and stir in the butter and Parmesan cheese. Serve very hot.

ZUPPA DI FINOCCHI

FENNEL SOUP

This is the perfect soup to eat after several heavy meals as the fennel has marvelous digestive properties. So if you have gotten to the point where you really can't face anything rich, but want to eat something which is soothing and original, try this easy soup.

SERVES 4–6

5 large, round, crunchy fennel bulbs
3 large cloves garlic, finely chopped
a handful of finely chopped fresh parsley
1¼ cups olive oil
salt and pepper
4 slices stale white bread

OX-DRAWN CART *The huge white oxen draw home forage — an evening scene unaltered in centuries of farming.*

Remove the outer parts of the fennel bulbs and slice the tender white interior into fine, neat strips. Put into a pan with the garlic, parsley, oil, and a pinch of salt. Fry gently for about 6 minutes, stirring and turning.

Cover with 5 cups cold water or chicken stock if you want a soup with a less gentle flavor. Bring to a boil, then reduce the heat and simmer slowly until the fennel falls to pieces. Taste and season very generously. Meanwhile, broil-toast the bread in the oven.

Place the toast in the bottom of the soup tureen. Pour the soup over it and serve at once.

MINESTRA DI RISO, LATTE E CASTAGNE

CHESTNUT, MILK, AND RICE SOUP

Most people either love or hate chestnuts, so perhaps this isn't the best choice for a dinner party or supper where you don't know your guests' tastes too well. If you are a chestnut person, like me, you will love this delicious and very nourishing soup. Its consistency is not unlike creamy oatmeal — or even rice pudding.

SERVES 4

7 oz fresh chestnuts
salt
⅔ cup short-grain rice
2½ cups milk
2 tablespoons unsalted butter

Pierce the chestnuts with a fork, put them in a saucepan, cover with lukewarm water, and boil for 5−8 minutes. Drain, then remove the shell and the soft inner skin. Place in a large saucepan with about 5 cups salted water and boil over medium heat for 2½ hours until the nuts are disintegrating and the liquid halved.

Add the rice and cook for about 12 minutes, until the rice is half cooked, then add the milk and butter. Cook until the soup is very thick and creamy, then season.

ACQUACOTTA

EGG, TOMATO, AND MUSHROOM SOUP

Literally meaning 'cooked water,' this is an ancient recipe from Tuscany consisting of mushrooms cooked with garlic, oil, and tomatoes — the resulting mixture is diluted to soup texture and poured into each plate or soup bowl where slices of coarse toasted bread have been laid to absorb excess liquid. The soup is finished off with grated cheese and eggs to make it more nourishing. Don't be put off by the name: the flavor is delicate, but truly delicious, as ceps are the most flavorful of all mushrooms.

SERVES 4

1 lb fresh porcini (ceps), or other wild mushrooms
4 tablespoons olive oil
2 cloves garlic, slightly crushed
salt and pepper
1 cup peeled, seeded fresh ripe tomatoes, or
canned tomatoes, seeded
8 thin slices stale white bread
3 eggs
2 heaping tablespoons Parmesan cheese, freshly grated

Clean the mushrooms, trim and wash carefully, dry them thoroughly, then slice. Heat the olive oil in a wide, deep 1½−2 quarts saucepan. Add the garlic and fry until golden, then add the mushrooms.

Season with salt and pepper and cook for about 15 minutes, then add the tomatoes. Stir in 4½ cups salted boiling water, cover and simmer until the mushrooms are completely soft, about 10 minutes.

Meanwhile, toast the bread in the oven until crisp. Place 2 slices in the bottom of each soup plate or bowl. Beat the eggs with the Parmesan cheese in a soup tureen and as soon as the soup is ready, pour it over the eggs and cheese. Beat again to scramble the eggs, then ladle it out over the bread.

TUSCAN FARMSTEAD *The remote Tuscan hills are sparsely dotted with farmsteads like this one nestling on the borders of a dark wood.*

MINESTRONE ALLA LIGURE

LIGURIAN MINESTRONE

Lots of fresh herbs and a flavorful rosemary pesto go into this delicious Ligurian soup.

SERVES 6

⅓ cup dried cannellini, haricot, or navy beans, soaked
overnight and brought back to a
boil twice
olive oil
1 large white onion, finely chopped
3 sticks celery, finely chopped
1 large slice Parma ham or other prosciutto crudo, cut
into thin strips
1 small cabbage — white is best for color —
finely shredded
2 large carrots, scraped, and finely chopped
6 large spinach leaves, trimmed, and washed
6 large dark green lettuce leaves, washed and chopped
1 generous tablespoon tomato paste
5 cups good chicken or vegetable stock
1 large clove garlic
a handful of fresh parsley leaves
2 small sprigs fresh rosemary
2 heaping tablespoons Parmesan cheese, freshly grated
plus extra for serving
¼ small dried red chili pepper
8 oz preferably wide pasta, e.g. lasagnette or
tagliatelle, broken into 3-inch lengths

Put 3 tablespoons olive oil in a 2 quart saucepan. Add the onion, celery, and prosciutto and sauté gently until the onion is transparent.

Add the beans, cabbage, carrots, spinach, lettuce, and tomato paste. Stir and cook these gently while heating the stock. Pour in the stock and stir. Cover and simmer for about 1½ hours, adding more stock if it seems needed.

Meanwhile, put garlic, parsley, rosemary, Parmesan, and chili into a mortar and pound to a paste. Push this pesto mixture through a sieve and set aside. (Alternatively, use a food processor, then sieve.)

Toss the pasta into the soup and cook until tender, then stir in the pesto mixture. Stir and allow to stand for a few minutes. Ladle out into bowls, cover with grated cheese, and serve immediately.

TORTELLINI IN BRODO

TORTELLINI IN A CLEAR SOUP

This is the most classic of all the soups from Emilia Romagna: the rich chicken stock has delicate handmade pasta parcels filled with ground meat that float on the surface. Making tortellini is an art; on your first practice run you might do better to use a 2-egg quantity of pasta and half the filling.

SERVES 6

CHICKEN STOCK
½ an average-sized chicken
1 lb stewing beef
1 large carrot, scraped
1 onion
2 sticks celery, trimmed
a handful of fresh parsley leaves
2 small cabbage leaves
salt and pepper
PASTA
2 cups all-purpose flour
3 large eggs
FILLING
⅓ cup cubed raw rump steak
⅓ cup cubed raw turkey breast
2 tablespoons butter
⅓ cup chopped mortadella sausage
⅓ cup chopped Parma ham or other prosciutto crudo
2 eggs
a pinch of grated nutmeg
1¼ cups freshly grated Parmesan cheese

To make the stock, put all the ingredients in the bottom of a soup pot, seasoning to taste with salt and pepper. Cover with about 3 quarts cold water and bring to a boil. Cover and simmer gently for about 3 hours. Check seasoning, strain twice, and leave to cool overnight.

The next day, make the pasta. Put the flour onto the table in a mound, make a hollow in the center with your fist. Break the eggs into the hollow. Keeping your fingers stiff, mix the eggs into the flour, then knead together.

Work the dough thoroughly for 15–20 minutes. It should be quite stiff, but golden yellow, elastic, and smooth. Cover with a damp clean cloth and leave to rest.

Meanwhile, make the filling. Cook the steak and turkey together in the butter over a low heat for 10 minutes. Cool, then mince twice with the mortadella and prosciutto. Mix in the eggs, nutmeg, salt and pepper, and 1¼ cups of the cheese. Set aside.

Roll out the pasta as thinly as possible, fold it in half and roll it again. Continue in this way until it snaps at the fold as you roll it. When you hear the snap it is ready to use. Roll it out again very thinly and cut it into 1½-inch circles with a pastry cutter or overturned wine glass.

Place a tiny mound of filling in the center of each circle, fold in half, and press the edges together tightly to prevent the filling escaping during cooking. When they are all folded securely, shape into crescents. Take each one and twist it around your index finger, secure the ends together tightly (moistened with a little cold water if necessary) and slide the completed tortellini off the end of your finger. Lay them out in neat rows on floured dish cloths, without overlapping. There may be filling left over – it depends on how good you become at rolling the pasta thinly.

Bring the broth to a boil. Slide the tortellini in and cook for 2–3 minutes. Serve at once with the remaining cheese sprinkled on top. I always drink, and recommend, a generous bottle of Lambrusco with this dish.

COMMUNAL SUPPER *The older generation get together for a special evening meal al fresco, accompanied by plenty of good local wine.*

ZUPPA DI ZUCCHINE

ZUCCHINI SOUP

This summer soup of zucchini, fresh basil, eggs, olive oil, bread, and cheese is a specialty of the southern province of Naples. Here the black soil along the coast supports a profusion of vegetables. Very fresh zucchini, with glossy skins, are crucial — and also young tender ones. Their maximum size should be 6 inches long by $1\frac{1}{2}$ inches diameter and when they are cut the seeds should be small. The quality of the vegetables will make the difference between a good soup and a tasteless one.

SERVES 4

5 very fresh zucchini, washed and trimmed
3 tablespoons olive oil
salt and pepper
2 large eggs
3 heaped tablespoons Parmesan cheese, freshly grated
3 tablespoons finely chopped fresh parsley
8 fresh basil leaves, finely chopped
8 slices stale white bread

Cut the unpeeled zucchini into neat small squares. Heat the oil in a saucepan, add the zucchini and fry gently together, turning frequently, for about 2 minutes.

Pour 5 cups cold water (or stock) over the zucchini, season with salt and pepper, and stir well. Cover, bring to a boil, then simmer for 45 minutes.

Beat the eggs in a bowl with the cheese and the herbs. Pour into the hot soup, beat through to scramble the eggs, and remove from the heat. Toast the bread and lay 2 slices in each soup bowl. Ladle the slightly cooled soup over the bread and serve.

PANCOTTO CON RUCOLA E PATATE

ARUGULA AND POTATO SOUP

This recipe from Apulia dates back to the Daunian civilization 2,500 years ago. It's one of the simplest soups, but bursts with flavor and with a lovely texture. The arugula is said to purify the blood.

SERVES 4

1 lb potatoes, peeled and thickly sliced
1 lb arugula or trimmed spinach
salt
8 slices stale white bread
4–6 tablespoons olive oil
1 small dried red chili pepper
2 cloves garlic, sliced into thin strips

Cover the potatoes with about 6 cups cold water. Bring to a boil and cook for 10 minutes. Meanwhile, wash and trim the arugula.

Add the arugula to the potatoes (coarsely chopped if the leaves are large, although it isn't traditional to do so!). Spinach doesn't have quite the same pungent taste as rocket, but it nevertheless makes a popular soup. Continue to cook the soup, stirring occasionally, until the potatoes are mushy. Season with salt and pepper, then add the bread. Stir the soup and pour it into a soup tureen.

Heat the oil in a pan, add the garlic and the chili, and sauté for about 8 minutes, then discard the chili. Pour the oil and garlic over the soup, stir once, and serve at once.

FRESHLY BAKED LOAVES *Straight from a wood-burning oven, the hot loaves are set out to cool on a cloth.*

PANE COTTO CON ALLORO

BREAD AND CHEESE SOUP

This soup crops up all over the country in various forms and has its roots in times of poverty when nothing was ever wasted, not even the leftover stale bread. It is a nourishing soup which can be thrown together quickly, though somewhat spartan for modern tastes. You might prefer to start with stock.

SERVES 4

salt
2 fresh bay leaves or 1 dried bay leaf
5 tablespoons olive oil
8 stale white bread rolls, broken into smallish pieces
8 tablespoons pecorino cheese, freshly grated

Bring 5 cups water to a boil with a pinch of salt. Add the fresh bay leaves or dried leaf and the oil. Stir and simmer for about 5 minutes. Throw in the bread and stir. Pour out into a soup tureen and sprinkle the cheese over the top.

JOTA

HEARTY WINTER SOUP

This is the perfect sort of soup to eat on really cold winter days. I like to prepare it in time to serve when friends return from a trek in the forest through the snow. Nothing else is necessary after a couple of bowlfuls, except maybe a dish of baked apples or some sliced oranges. A good rich red wine like a Merlot complements the flavors perfectly.

SERVES 6

1¼ cups dried borlotti, pinto, kidney, or cannellini beans, soaked overnight
⅔ cup diced fresh bacon
2 tablespoons vegetable oil or pork drippings
1 tablespoon all-purpose flour
4 tablespoons lard or shortening
1 large onion, very finely chopped

½ teaspoon dried sage
2 cloves garlic, very finely chopped
a handful of fresh parsley, very finely chopped
5 tablespoons polenta flour (or cornmeal)
⅓ cup smoked bacon or pancetta
1¼ cups sauerkraut
salt

Drain the beans, put them in a pan, cover with water, and bring to a boil. After 10 minutes, drain, and rinse, then cover with about 6 cups cold water and the diced fresh bacon. Bring to a boil, cover and simmer slowly. Heat the oil or drippings and flour together to make a roux, then stir it into the beans. Continue to cook for about 30 minutes.

In another skillet sauté the lard or shortening, onion, sage, garlic, and parsley together until amalgamated. Add the polenta flour or cornmeal to the lard mixture, then add this to the beans. Stir and simmer for another 30 minutes. Fry the bacon or pancetta until the fat is running and sizzling, add the sauerkraut and stir together, then mix into the soup. Taste for seasoning and serve at once.

ZUPPA DI FAGIOLI

BEAN SOUP

The secret of success is in using fresh beans. If you really cannot get hold of any, the dried variety will have to do, but the flavor won't be the same. Always bring the beans to a full boil after soaking them. Wash and drain them, then use as fresh. The onion is not necessary when using fresh beans, but essential when using dry ones.

SERVES 4

4 cups fresh borlotti or pinto beans, or 1¾ cups dried, soaked overnight and drained
1 large onion, finely chopped
1 large stick celery, finely chopped
1¾ cups fresh parsley, finely chopped
about 3 tablespoons (¼ cup) olive oil
3 tablepoons finely chopped bacon or ham fat (preferably smoked)
2 tablespoons tomato paste
salt and pepper

Cover the fresh or soaked beans in cold water, bring to a boil, and simmer gently until soft. Dried beans will take about an hour. Mix the parsley, celery, and bacon or ham fat together very thoroughly to make a paste.

Heat the olive oil and fat in a deep saucepan, add the onion, celery and parsley mixture, and sauté together, until the onion is soft. Add the tomato paste and mix together, adding about 6 tablespoons of warm water to dilute the paste.

Drain the cooked beans, add to the pan and stir. Pour in enough boiling water to make the quantity of soup you require – about 4 cups. Add the water slowly and carefully so that you have just the right amount and don't finish up with a watery mess. Broil-toast the bread in the oven and place in the bottom of the soup tureen. Cook the soup, covered, for 10 minutes, then pour it over the bread and serve.

LA MES – CIUA

MIXED LEGUME SOUP

This very different soup is included for historical reasons. The original version contained only dried maize, chick peas, and beans, flavored with cheese – I have used fresh corn and added some flavoring ingredients. It is a specialty of La Spezia and the surrounding area – born out of a time when there was not enough flour to make bread, nor enough beans or dried maize to make a dish, and certainly no meat available to simply waste in a soup.

SERVES 6

1½ cups dried chick peas
1½ cups dried cannellini beans or
1½ cups dried butter beans
2 pinches baking soda
kernels from 3 corn cobs
salt and freshly ground black pepper

SACKFULS OF BEANS *The best and cheapest way of buying dried legumes in Italy is straight from the sack.*

5 cups stock
1 onion, finely chopped
4 cloves garlic, crushed
4 tablespoons tomato paste
freshly grated Parmesan cheese

Sort through the legumes, removing bad ones. Put the chick peas and the beans in separate large bowls, add a pinch of baking soda to each, cover with water and leave overnight. Also check the package instructions – modern varieties of chick peas cook faster than beans; with others the reverse is true.

The next day, drain the beans, wash, put in a large saucepan, and cover with more water. Boil quickly for 10 minutes. Drain and put them in a large saucepan with the onion, garlic, tomato paste, stock, and a pinch of salt, and bring to a boil. Drain and wash the chick peas, and put in a separate saucepan. Add salt and water and bring to a boil. After 10 minutes, add the corn kernels to the chick peas. Cook for about 30 minutes until the beans are mushy and the chick peas and corn are soft.

Pour the chick pea mixture into the beans with some of their liquid (you should have about 7½ cups). Season and cook gently for 15 minutes more. Each person should add freshly ground pepper and Parmesan cheese to taste.

CIPOLLATA

ONION AND TOMATO SOUP

This very simple tomato-flavored onion soup from Umbria is scented with fresh basil and enriched with golden-green olive oil. If you are using fresh tomatoes with a poor color, add a tablespoon of tomato paste.

SERVES 4

2¼ lb large yellow onions, thinly sliced
3 tablespoons ham fat, chopped
1 tablespoon olive oil
7 fresh basil leaves
salt and pepper
1 lb soft, fresh ripe tomatoes, chopped and sieved,
or passata
Parmesan cheese, freshly grated
2 large eggs, beaten

Cover the sliced onions with cold water and leave to soak overnight.

The next day, drain the onions. Sauté the ham fat and olive oil together for 5 minutes, then add the onions and basil and season with salt and pepper. Stir well, cover, and leave to steam slowly over lowest heat until the onions have softened but are not colored.

Stir in the sieved tomatoes and 4½ cups water. Cover and simmer for an additional 1½ hours. Remove from the heat, cover with Parmesan cheese, and quickly beat in the eggs. Serve as a thick and very substantial soup with toasted bread or bruschetta – bread grilled with oil and garlic – and plenty of robust red wine. Colli del Trasimeno is a good choice.

FAVATA

PORK AND FAVA BEAN SOUP

This is one of those thick, nutritious, and full-of-goodness, main-course soups which needs plenty of time cooking. Even if you leave it bubbling for a whole day or night, it will only become even tastier. Add the oil just before you serve the soup.

SERVES 6

2 cups dried fava or lima beans
2 lb small pork chops
10 oz Italian pork sausages
10 oz bacon
olive oil
a large pinch of mixed dried herbs
2 fresh tomatoes, peeled and chopped
1 stick celery, chopped
1 onion, chopped
1 carrot, chopped
¼ small cabbage, shredded
¼ bulb fennel, chopped
3 cloves garlic, crushed

Soak the beans overnight, then wash them. Put in a large pan, cover with water, and boil rapidly for 5 minutes. Drain and wash them, then cut each one through the skin, making a slit in each bean on one side only. Set aside.

Cut all the meats into small chunks and put in a large deep flameproof casserole with a little olive oil. Fry gently together until slightly browned, then add the herbs, tomatoes, celery, onion, and carrot. Pour over 3 quarts of water and bring to a slow, steady simmer.

When the vegetables are fairly tender, add the beans and all the remaining ingredients. Stir well, then cover and simmer slowly for 2½ hours. Remove from the heat, spoon into bowls, and stir in ½ tablespoon olive oil into each one. Serve with plenty of coarse country-style bread.

FAVATA

PASTA, PIZZA, RICE, POLENTA

Homemade pastas, delicately stuffed, delight the eye and the palate; pizza and polenta provide hearty, stick-to-the-ribs nourishment; and the humble rice grain is the foundation of some magnificent risottos.

TORTA RUSTICA *left (p 46)*
STRANGOLAPRIEVE *right (p 40)*

A PLATE OF PIPING HOT PASTA dressed with a rich, brightly-colored sauce is one of the most satisfying dishes I can think of. And surely nothing is more satisfying and warming in the winter than a slab of polenta surmounted by a gloriously rich stew. In summertime, savory pies, cakes, and pizza make mouthwatering companions for lunching al fresco. Then there is rice, that self-effacing, humble-looking grain which happens to be the key to magnificent dishes when combined with the right accompaniments — everything from eel to red wine and beans. For smaller appetites, these dishes will suffice as a meal in themselves, but traditionally they are only one dish in the procession of courses — following an antipasto of cured meats and pickles and preceding a simple dish of meat and vegetables, or fish, or cheese and egg dishes.

In almost all cases, the recipes for pasta in this section call for the pasta to be made by hand. This could cause a few problems for beginners, but after just a little practice I can assure you that you will find it very easy. When you first make pasta, the main thing is not to worry too much about what it looks like! Basic rules apply: make it all about the same thickness so that it will cook evenly, and for the same reason, make the separate pieces roughly the same size as each other. Seal pasta parcels with great care so the filling won't escape.

Polenta, or cornmeal, is now widely available and I am quite confident that it will become extremely popular. If you buy pre-cooked polenta which is in a package, the cooking procedure will be much faster and easier — so use this kind for any recipe which involves a short cooking or baking time. Loose-pack polenta must be cooked very slowly with somebody constantly stirring to prevent disastrous sticking and disgusting lumpiness. You can buy yellow or white polenta, and it is entirely a matter of personal taste which you choose, although the experts say that the white version is better with fish than the yellow.

The eventual texture of the polenta is also very much a personal taste and it may help to imagine that you are making porridge. Some like it runnier, some like it very much thicker, and it does all depend upon what you are serving it with. Polenta on its own is nothing to get excited about, but just try it with slices of gooey, very ripe Gorgonzola, so that the very hot polenta melts the cheese into an amazing, delicious taste experience, and you will never look at bread and cheese again! Leftover polenta is allowed to cool and solidify completely, then is sliced into thickish strips and fried in olive oil until hot and crisp, or grilled until charred on the outside.

Once you have made it half-a-dozen times, you will begin to experiment with accompaniments and different textures until you find your own favorite. As a child, I was always given polenta in a soup plate, covered with warm milk, and finished off with a pat of butter — I have yet to taste anything quite so good.

CASUMZIEEI AMPEZZANI

BEET PASTA POCKETS
WITH POPPY SEEDS

This unusual type of ravioli from the Veneto has a filling of beets and ricotta cheese and is tossed with poppy seeds, butter, and grated cheese.

SERVES 4

*1 lb, 2 oz fresh beets, boiled in salted water
until tender
9 tablespoons unsalted butter
⅓ cup ricotta cheese
salt
4 large eggs
about 1 cup fresh white bread crumbs
3 cups minus 4 tablespoons all-purpose flour
¾ cup plus 1–2 tablespoons milk
4 teaspoons poppy seeds
Parmesan cheese, freshly grated*

Peel and mash the beets to a soft pulp. Melt about half the butter in a saucepan, add the mashed beets and stir together. Add the ricotta cheese and mix it in thoroughly. Remove from the heat, pour into a bowl, and add 2 eggs, a little salt, and enough bread crumbs to make a fairly thick, sticky mixture.

Make a smooth dough by kneading together for about 10–15 minutes the flour, the remaining 2 eggs, and as much milk as is needed. Then roll it out very thinly and cut it into equal-sized circles with a pastry cutter or an overturned wine glass. Put a little of the beet filling in the center of each circle, fold it in half, and firmly press closed with your fingertips.

Bring a very large pan of water to a boil, add the ravioli, and cook them for 4–5 minutes until they float to the surface. Scoop them out with a large slotted spoon and place them in a warmed bowl.

Meanwhile, melt the remaining butter in a small pan. Pour the butter over the ravioli, scatter the poppy seeds and Parmesan cheese to taste over them, toss them very gently, and serve at once.

TORTELLI CON PATATE

PASTA POCKETS
WITH A POTATO FILLING

These parcels of very simple handmade pasta from Emilia Romagna are filled with a potato stuffing.

SERVES 4

*3 cups plus four tablespoons all-purpose flour
1 medium-sized egg
salt
7 tablespoons unsalted butter, cubed
1 cup Parmesan cheese, freshly grated*
FILLING
*1 lb, 12 oz potatoes, peeled
1 large onion, finely chopped
4 cloves garlic, finely chopped
⅓ cup bacon or pancetta, finely chopped
salt and freshly ground black pepper
⅔ cup ricotta cheese
a pinch of grated nutmeg
a handful of Parmesan cheese, freshly grated*

To make the filling, boil the potatoes until soft, mash them thoroughly, and set aside. Process the onion, garlic, and bacon or pancetta together in a food processor until mushy but not puréed, then sauté until the fat runs and the onion is soft and transparent.

Stir the mashed potatoes and add plenty of black pepper. Mix in the ricotta cheese and nutmeg, Parmesan cheese, salt, and more pepper. Mix thoroughly and set aside to cool completely.

Put the flour and a pinch of salt in a mound, make a hole in the center with your fist, break in the egg, and add enough water to make a smooth elastic dough. You will need to knead it for about 20 minutes.

When the dough feels elastic and manageable, roll it out as thinly as possible. Cut into rectangles about $1\frac{1}{2} \times 2\frac{3}{4}$ inches. Put a little filling in the center of each one and fold it in half. Seal the 3 open edges with a fork.

Bring a large saucepan of salted water to a boil, add the pasta, and cook for about 4 minutes. Scoop out with a slotted spoon and transfer to a warm bowl. Scatter the butter over the pasta and toss carefully. Sprinkle with Parmesan cheese and serve.

STRANGOLAPRIEVE

PRIEST STRANGLERS

The story behind this delicious dish is that it was reserved for the occasions when the priest came to call. Priests being notoriously either underfed or very greedy, they would chow into this dish so voraciously that they would virtually choke themselves. There is another story which claims that the idea *was* to choke the priest!

SERVES 6

4 cups all-purpose flour
1 cup semolina
salt and pepper
1 lb fresh ripe tomatoes, cut in half
a handful of fresh parsley
4 sprigs of fresh basil
1 large stick celery with leaves, quartered
1 large onion, quartered
4 tablespoons unsalted butter
Parmesan cheese, freshly grated

Pour the flour and semolina together in a mound. Plunge your clenched fist into the mound, then add a pinch of salt and just enough warm water to allow you to begin kneading. (The emphasis here is on elbow grease rather than more liquid.)

Knead, roll, and fold until you have a smooth and elastic dough, no softer than average bread dough – if anything somewhat stiffer. It will take 20–30 minutes. Cover the dough with a damp cloth and leave to rest.

Put the tomatoes, parsley, basil, celery, onion, oil, and a seasoning of salt and pepper into a saucepan, cover and simmer slowly in their own juices until the tomatoes fall apart. Leave to cool, then push it through a vegetable mill or sieve into another pan. Stir and keep warm until required.

Roll out the rested dough into sections no larger than your little finger. Cut each section into 5 or 6 pieces, and rock them to and fro on the table to hollow them out slightly, pressing down very hard with your thumb. Bring a large saucepan of salted water to a boil, add the pasta, and cook for 2–3 minutes, scooping them out as soon as they return to the surface. Pour over the warm tomato sauce and add the butter and plenty of Parmesan cheese. Toss it all together and serve at once.

PANSOTTI AU PREBOGGION CON SALSA DI NOCI

WILD HERB PASTA POCKETS WITH WALNUT SAUCE

Preboggion is a handful of mixed, wild, edible herbs, widely sold in all the main Genoese markets. Traditionally, preboggion must include wild borage, lovage, dog's tooth, sorrel, wild chicory, wild onion, and wild chervil but can also include anything else you come across! To achieve the same effect, use as many fresh garden herbs (and wild ones if possible) as you have available. Both the pasta pockets and the sauce have a wonderful flavor.

SERVES 4

FILLING

2 lb very young trimmed spinach mixed with 8 oz various fresh herbs (about 4 cups)
⅔ cup ricotta cheese
½ cup Parmesan cheese, freshly grated
2 eggs, lightly beaten
1 clove garlic, finely chopped
salt

SAUCE

1 lb unshelled walnuts
3 slices stale bread, soaked in cold water until mushy
1 clove garlic
salt
4 tablespoons sour milk
4 tablespoons olive oil
3 tablespoons unsalted butter
8 tablespoons Parmesan cheese, grated

PASTA

3 cups less 4 tablespoons all-purpose flour
½ cup cold water
2 teaspoons white wine

TO SERVE

Parmesan cheese, freshly grated
butter

HOMEMADE RAVIOLI *These homemade ravioli look dainty enough to be the handiwork of a seamstress!*

To make the filling, cook the herbs and spinach together in a pan of boiling salted water. Drain and squeeze between your hands, then mince in a blender or food processor to a smooth green goo. Mix in the ricotta and Parmesan cheeses, eggs, and garlic. Season to taste with salt.

To make the sauce, crack the nuts, then blanch them in boiling water for 30 seconds to loosen the inner skins. Peel off the skins. Remove the bread from the water and squeeze dry in your fist. Grind the nuts in a blender or herb mill – this produces a finer texture than a food processor – with the garlic and a pinch of salt. (Using a food processor you will need to pound the nuts in a mortar afterwards.) Gradually add the squeezed-out bread with a little sour milk if it is too stiff. Process until smooth, then sieve into a bowl. Stir in the sour milk and the oil (more or less depending upon what consistency you prefer), taste and adjust seasoning. Keep the sauce at room temperature.

To make the pasta, pour the flour in a mound. Make a hole in the center with your fist and pour in the water and wine. Combine the flour with the liquid, knead to a smooth white dough, and set aside to rest for a little while under a clean, damp cloth.

Roll out the dough as thinly as possible and cut into triangles measuring about 3 inches on each side. Put a tiny amount of filling in the middle of each one, fold over to make a smaller triangle and press tightly closed with your finger tips (they must be well-sealed or the filling will fall out during cooking).

Cook the pasta in boiling salted water for about 4 minutes, drain, and pour over the sauce, tossing carefully so as not to split them. Serve with grated Parmesan cheese and butter dotted about on top.

CAVATIEDDI CON LA RUCOLA

TINY PASTA SHELLS WITH ARUGULA

Cavatieddi look like small pasta seashells. In this recipe they are cooked with arugula to give them a distinctive flavor, then tossed with a plain tomato sauce. Both the red, white, and green colors and the texture of the dish are most attractive.

SERVES 4

½ cup semolina
1½ cups white flour
tepid, slightly salted water
1 large onion, finely chopped
2 sticks celery, finely chopped
1 clove garlic, finely chopped
1 carrot, finely chopped
2 tablespoons olive oil
2½ cups tomato sauce
salt and pepper
1 lb arugula, washed, or spinach, trimmed
pecorino or Parmesan cheese, freshly grated, to taste

Sift the semolina and flour together twice. Pour them into a mound. Plunge your fist into the center of the pile, pour in a little tepid salty water. Begin to knead together — you are trying to achieve the same consistency as bread dough, stiffer, but no softer. After about 25 minutes you should have reached the right texture. Cover the dough with a damp dish cloth.

To form the pasta shapes, break off pieces of the dough, keeping the rest covered. Roll each piece into a cylinder about 12–16 inches long. Each cylinder should be no thicker than ¾ inch and each piece of dough must be worked quickly to prevent it from drying out. When the cylinder of dough is the right length and thickness, cut it into discs with a sharp knife. Then poke the point of the knife into the center of each disc and roll it up on itself, to make it slightly concave. This used to be done by rolling the pasta several times along the wood grain of a rough table top, which also marked the outside. The pasta should look like small seashells.

When all the dough has been rolled and shaped, leave the cavatieddi uncovered to dry in the air overnight. Turn over to dry the underside. When they are completely dried out, they are ready for cooking in water.

The next day, fry the onion, celery, garlic, and carrot in the oil until the onion is soft and transparent. Pour in the tomato sauce and stir. Season with salt and pepper, cover, and leave to simmer for about 30 minutes.

Put the arugula in a saucepan, cover with cold water and a pinch of salt, and boil briefly until tender. Double the quantity of water, return to a boil, and add the pasta. Cook until tender.

Drain the pasta and arugula together, transfer to a warmed bowl, pour over the tomato sauce. Toss together thoroughly, scatter pecorino cheese over it all and serve.

An alternative is to sauce the cavatieddi quite simply with a half cup of olive oil in which you have fried 3 cloves of garlic and 2 salted anchovies. The oil must be of the very best quality.

PASTA CON SUGO DI LEPRE

PASTA WITH HARE SAUCE

In Sardinia, wide use is made of Pasta Asciutta (literally translated as dry pasta, it actually means pasta which is boiled, drained, and tossed with a sauce). In the hunting season, the sauces are often made with wild boar, hare, or other locally shot game. Traditionally, the blood is an essential part of this dish and the ideal would be to use an animal which you have shot and hung yourself. You can then skin and gut as you require. However, if you do not want to do it yourself, order a hare or rabbit in advance from your butcher and ask him to cut it up and reserve the blood for you.

SERVES 4

3 slices fatty bacon
⅓ cup olive oil
1 small hare or rabbit, divided into 8 pieces,
with its blood
2 large onions, thinly sliced
2 large cloves garlic, crushed
1 tablespoon all purpose flour
1 standard-sized bottle red wine
salt and pepper
a few cloves
a large pinch of cinnamon
a large pinch of dried mixed herbs
bouquet garni
4 oz spaghetti
pecorino sardo or Parmesan cheese, freshly grated
to taste

Fry the bacon in deep flameproof casserole with the oil, then add the hare and brown it all over. Add the onions and garlic and sauté for a few minutes until the onions are golden and soft.

Sprinkle the flour in and cook for 5 minutes, then pour in the wine. Add the salt and pepper to taste, the cloves, cinnamon, dried mixed herbs, and bouquet garni. Stir it all together, cover and simmer for about 1½ hours.

Bring a large pan of salted water to a boil, add the spaghetti and cook until al dente (tender but still firm). Drain and transfer to a warm bowl.

Pour the sauce from the hare over the pasta, toss together thoroughly with as much grated cheese as you like. Arrange into 4 portions on plates and put 2 pieces of hare on top of each pile of spaghetti. Serve at once. Alternatively, serve the spaghetti with the sauce and serve the hare as a second course with vegetables and potatoes or salad.

Instead of spaghetti, you might like to try a wide ribbon noodle. This is traditional in Tuscany, although it is rather unusual to find a celebrated pasta dish in the northern part of the country. In Pappardelle con la lepre, wide home-made noodles are served with a hare and red wine sauce rather similar to this one.

STRINGS OF RED ONIONS *This type of onion makes the colorful topping for* FITASCETTA *(p 48).*

DAWN IN AN OLIVE GROVE *(p 44) The proprietor in his well-tended grove, carries a gun to scare off marauding birds.*

LASAGNE INCASSETTATE

OVEN-BAKED LASAGNE

This most traditional and old-fashioned layered lasagne comes from the Marche region of Italy on the Adriatic coast. In other areas, the pasta, sauce, and cheeses are served separately so each person can add as much or as little as they like. The cream is a modern addition.

SERVES 4

3 cups all-purpose plain flour
3 eggs
1½ tablespoons olive oil
salt
FILLING AND CONDIMENTS
1¾ oz pancetta or ham fat (preferably smoked)
5 tablespoons unsalted butter
1 onion, chopped
2 fat garlic cloves, finely chopped
8 oz raw veal, pork, or lamb, finely chopped
8 oz chicken giblets
1 chicken breast, chopped into cubes (save breast bone)
⅔ cup dry white wine
1½ tablespoons chicken livers, cleaned and chopped
1 cup heavy cream
pinch of dried oregano
5 tablespoons parsley, finely chopped
salt and pepper
½ cup Parmesan cheese, freshly grated
⅔ cup Gruyère or Swiss cheese, grated
1 small white truffle (optional)

Make the pasta, adding the eggs to the flour with salt and just enough oil to make it smooth. Knead very thoroughly for 5 minutes in a food processor, 15–20 minutes by hand.

To make the filling, fry the pancetta or ham fat in half the butter then add the onion and garlic. After 5 minutes, add the meat and fry for 5 minutes. Add the chicken giblets, chopped breast and breast bone, and wine and cook for 5 minutes. Cover and simmer very slowly for about 1 hour, adding water if necessary.

Roll out the pasta several times, folding it in half and rolling it again each time. Keep doing this until there is an audible snap as you roll the pin over the fold and push the air out. The pasta is then ready: alternatively, use a pasta machine, which rolls and rerolls thinly.

Roll out the dough as thinly as possible; this is important as it puffs slightly when cooked. Then cut it into wide strips (like wide tagliatelle). Bring a large pan of salted water to a boil. Cook the pasta a few strips at a time, until only half cooked (about 3 minutes), drain it, and plunge it into a sink of cold water. If making the lasagne ahead, drain it again, and lay it out on dish cloths to dry, making sure the strips don't touch.

To complete the filling, remove the chicken giblets and discard all the bones. Chop the meat and return it to the pan. Add the chicken liver, cream, oregano, and parsley, season and cook for 5 more minutes.

To assemble, butter a 1½ quart dish and arrange a layer of pasta in the bottom with a little sauce and some of each cheese. Continue layer by layer, adding a little butter, until everything is used, spooning the remaining liquid over the top and ending with a layer of cheese. If you are using the truffle, shave it lightly over the finished dish. Dot with any remaining butter. Bake in a 350°F oven for 20–30 minutes.

TORTA RUSTICA

RUSTIC SAVORY CAKE

Essentially this is a southern Italian savory pizza cake! It's ideally suited to outdoor events such as wine or oil harvest or fruit picking because the filling is inside the dough. It's prepared for peasant festivities, with a variety of fillings – this is the most classic.

SERVES 6

3 cups less 4 tablespoons all-purpose flour
salt and pepper
3 tablespoons olive oil plus extra for frying
3 tablespoons dry white wine
8 oz ham, sliced very thick and cubed (about 1½ cups)
1 cup ricotta cheese
2 cups mozzarella cheese, cubed
1 cup caciocavallo cheese, cubed
2 large eggs, beaten
1 tablespoon sugar

Mix the flour with a pinch of salt, the oil, and the wine and just enough water to bind it, about $\frac{1}{2}$ cup. Knead to a smooth elastic dough, then roll it out thinly.

Oil a round cake pan large enough to take the dough and all the other ingredients — an $8\frac{1}{2}$-inch springform pan is ideal. Line the pan with two-thirds of the rolled-out dough, pressing it up the sides.

Fry the ham in a little oil, remove from the heat and stir in the 3 cheeses. Remove 1 teaspoon of beaten eggs and set it aside. Stir the rest of the eggs into the ham and cheese, add a little pepper, stir once more and tip into the lined cake pan, smoothing it with a spoon.

Slice the remaining one-third of the dough into wide strips and lay them across the filled cake pan in a tight lattice, covering the filling completely. Press the edges together tightly all the way around. Brush with the reserved spoonful of egg, sprinkle with the sugar, and bake in a 350°F oven for about 45 minutes. Serve either cold or warm at any picnic.

TRUCK LADEN WITH LEMON AND CHILI BRANCHES *The fruit and chilies still on the branch could not provide a more typically Mediterranean shock of color.*

FITASCETTA

RED ONION PIZZA

Serve this flat, fragrant, savory dough ring, one of the earliest types of pizza, with a selection of Italian cold cuts, and plenty of icy white wine.

SERVES 4

PIZZA

2$\frac{3}{4}$ cups all-purpose flour

a pinch of salt

$\frac{1}{2}$ oz fresh yeast, diluted in a little warm water, left to froth up in a warm place

1 lb Spanish onions, finely sliced and soaked in cold water for about 10 minutes

2 tablespoons unsalted butter

salt and pepper

olive oil

a large sprig of fresh rosemary

1 tablespoon light brown sugar or 1 teaspoon coarse salt

Pour out all but 3 tablespoons of the flour. Make a hollow in the center with your fist and put the salt and yeast in the hollow. Mix together and knead with as much water as it takes to make a smooth elastic bread dough. Rub the remaining flour over the work surface and your hands. When the dough is smooth and well-worked, cover it with a cloth and leave in a warm place to double in size — an hour or more.

Drain the onions and sauté them very gently in the butter as slowly as you can — until they become transparent. Season with salt and pepper.

Knead the dough briefly with a little warm water, roll it out like a long sausage, then form it into a circle, keeping the middle hole as large as possible. Oil an ovenproof tray and place the circle on it, flattening it slightly.

Spread the onions all over the dough, making sure they don't drop down into the middle hole! Break the rosemary into pieces and stick them into the dough at even intervals. Scatter the sugar or salt over the top and bake in a 400°F oven for 30 minutes. Eat warm or cold.

PITTA CHICCULIATA

CALABRIAN PIZZA

This is a pizza with the filling on the inside. Fillings inside can be all kinds of things, from basil, tomato, and olive to sausages and cheese.

SERVES 4

4½ cups all-purpose flour plus extra for kneading
a pinch of salt
¾ oz fresh yeast, diluted in a little warm water,
left to froth up in a warm place
1 large clove garlic
olive oil
about 1 cup tomato sauce
2 tablespoons salted anchovy fillets, washed
⅓ cup salted capers, washed
½ cup black olives, stoned and chopped
1 cup tuna in oil
⅓ cup lard or shortening, cubed
2 large egg yolks, beaten

Put 4 cups plus 4 tablespoons of the flour on your work surface. Make a hollow in the center with your fist and put the salt and yeast in the hollow. Mix together and knead with as much water as it takes to make a smooth elastic bread dough, rubbing flour over the work surface and your hands. When the dough is smooth and well-worked, cover it with a cloth and leave in a warm place to rise until it has doubled in size.

Meanwhile, sauté the garlic in a little oil, add the tomato sauce and a little more oil, cook briefly, then remove from the heat. Add the anchovies, capers, and olives, then flake in the tuna and mix well.

When the dough has doubled, push it flat on the table and knead in three-quarters of the lard or shortening. Set aside a teaspoonful of beaten egg and knead the remainder into the dough. Knead very thoroughly, then tear off one-third of the dough piece, so you have a big and a smaller piece.

Oil a 10-inch springform or other round pan and line it with the bigger piece of dough. Fill it with tomato mixture

MAKING TOMATO PASTE *This traditional method of drying sieved tomatoes in the sun achieves a dense and intensely 'tomato-y' concentrate.*

and cover with the second piece of dough, rolled out thinly. Pinch the edges together carefully, brush with the reserved beaten egg and the remaining piece of fat, rendered, and leave to rise in a warm place for 30 minutes. Bake in a 350°F oven for 25–30 minutes. Serve the pizza hot, perhaps with green salad.

RISOTTO RUSTI

RED WINE AND BORLOTTI RISOTTO

In Lombardy they know just about everything you might need to know about risotto and red wine. This wonderfully rustic risotto is made with lard, beans, onions, and red wine — some of my personal favorites are Botticino, Buttafuoco, or Oltrepò Pavese Barbera.

SERVES 4

4½ cups or more vegetable, chicken,
or beef stock
7 tablespoons lard, butter, or diced ham fat
1 large onion, finely chopped
1½ cups medium-grain rice
¾ cup Italian red wine
salt and pepper
1 cup cooked borlotti or pinto beans
(fresh, dried, or canned)
4 tablespoons unsalted butter
⅓ cup Parmesan cheese, freshly grated

Heat the stock to a slow simmer. In a large pan, heat the lard, butter, or ham fat until sizzling softly, then add the onion and cook gently until the onion is a transparent blond color and soft. Add the rice and sauté it carefully, turning it so it is coated in fat.

Pour in the red wine, stir, and cook for 5 minutes. Season with salt and pepper. Add the stock, and the beans alternately, stirring in a ladleful of stock then a large spoonful of beans. Allow the rice to absorb the broth before adding any more. Continue until the rice has almost cooked, about 25 minutes from the time of adding it to the onion. Take off the heat and stir in the butter and Parmesan cheese. Cover and leave to rest for 2–3 minutes, then turn out onto a serving dish and serve.

RISO ALLA SICILIANA

SICILIAN RICE

This delicious rice dish brings together all the most typical flavors of Sicilian cuisine. It should be lukewarm when served but never refrigerated. You can add more tomatoes fried in olive oil and flavored with marjoram if you like. It's delicious served as part of a summer buffet with other vegetable dishes. As in many Sicilian dishes, it is the layering of the three main parts of the dish which is important, mixing them together would completely change the nature of the dish.

SERVES 4

1 large salted anchovy or 2 anchovy fillets
1½ cups long-grain rice
1 onion, finely chopped
about 5 tablespoons olive oil
1 tablespoon white wine vinegar
⅔ cup white wine
juice of 3 lemons
½ teaspoon mustard
½ teaspoon tomato paste
3 firm ripe tomatoes, halved, seeded, and cubed
½ cup black olives, pitted
large pinch of dried marjoram

Bring a large saucepan of salted water to a boil. Put a plate on top of the pan, covering the water. Lay the anchovy on the plate and mash it with a fork. It will dissolve smoothly with heat. When the anchovy has dissolved, remove the plate and add the rice to the water and cook until tender.

Meanwhile, in a small saucepan, sauté the onion in 2 tablespoons olive oil. When the onion is golden and soft, sprinkle the vinegar over it and allow it to evaporate for 2 minutes. Add the wine, lemon juice, mustard, anchovy, and tomato paste. Mix with great care, then sieve once to make a smooth sauce.

Drain the rice and spread it out on a warmed serving platter. Pour the sauce over it and sprinkle with a little salt and pepper. While the rice cools slightly, fry the tomato cubes quickly in about 3 tablespoons olive oil for 1 minute, then mix in the olives and the marjoram. Pour them over the rice and sauce, then serve.

BRUDERA

SAUSAGE—MEAT RISOTTO

It is impossible to make any of the many dishes of Italian peasant cuisine that use fresh pig's blood unless you live near a pig farmer or are brave enough to go to the slaughterhouse yourself. I know it sounds revolting, but I promise you the end result is delicious and very nutritious.

SERVES 4—6

about 1 lb wings, neck, gizzards, or
other chicken trimmings
1 lb pork ribs (as meaty as possible)
salt
1 onion, finely sliced
7 tablespoons butter
⅓ cup Italian sausage-meat
freshly ground black pepper
2 cups medium-grain Italian rice
½ cup fresh pig's blood,
at room temperature (optional)
Parmesan cheese, freshly grated, to serve

Put the chicken trimmings and the ribs in a large saucepan with a little salt and 6 cups water and bring to a slow boil, then simmer for about 2 hours. Remove meat and leave to cool; keep the stock hot.

Fry half the onion and half the butter with the sausage-meat. Scrape the meat off the pork ribs and chicken and mince it once, or chop very finely, then mix with the onion and sausage. Season with black pepper. Cover and simmer for 15 minutes.

Sauté the remaining half onion gently in the remaining butter until the onion is soft. Add the rice and stir well. Fry it lightly, then start adding the hot stock, a ladleful at a time, stirring it into the rice each time. After 15 minutes, stir in the blood, if using, or the cooked meats with the onion. (If you are using the blood do not add the meat at this stage.) Add a little more stock and cook for the final 5 minutes.

Turn out onto a platter, scatter the meat on top if not already added, and serve with plenty of Parmesan cheese. If you do use the blood, you will find the dish turns a lovely brick red color and changes completely in flavor. Serve with a good bottle of Barolo or Barbaresco.

RISO ALLA SICILIANA

RISI E BISATO

RISOTTO WITH EEL

This superb risotto, which is made with eel, comes from the Veneto. Serve it with a Piave Verduzzo.

SERVES 4

10 oz fresh eel (can be a fresh-water or sea fish)
a handful of fresh parsley leaves
2 cloves garlic
1 cup minus one tablespoon olive oil
salt
1 small bay leaf
2 teaspoons or more lemon juice
1½ cups risotto rice
3–3½ cups vegetable stock
black pepper, freshly ground
½ cup cooked green peas (optional)
lemon wedges to garnish

Skin, gut, and wash the eel then cut into short chunks. Chop the parsley and garlic together, put into a saucepan with the oil and heat gently. Add the eel to the pan and sprinkle with a little salt. Add the bay leaf and lemon juice, cover and cook for about 10 minutes.

Stir in the rice and half the broth, stir and continue to cook, adding more broth as soon as it is absorbed, until the rice is tender. Remove the pan from the heat, stir in plenty of freshly ground black pepper, and the cooked peas if using. Leave covered for 2 minutes.

To serve, spoon out into a mound or flattish cake shape on a serving dish. Garnish with lemon.

POLENTA SULLA SPIANATORA

POLENTA ON THE TABLE

The origins of this dish go way back in the dark mists of time, but maybe there is a place for the meaning behind the dish — now more than ever. The ritual arising from eating the food in this way is that gradually trenches and gullies open up in the polenta as everybody picks out the best bits, until at last the culmination of the meal is all the forks touching one another — a symbol of friendship and fraternity. The atmosphere surrounding this meal is very jovial and fun loving — try it for yourself and see. The best kind of table is one that is much battle-scarred and imbued with flavors of a thousand and one meals prepared and eaten on it.

SERVES 8

1 large onion, chopped
1 large carrot, chopped
1 large stick celery, chopped
3 cloves garlic, peeled and chopped
a handful of mixed fresh parsley and basil leaves
5 tablespoons olive oil
4½ cups tomato sauce
16–20 sausages (preferably Italian)
salt and pepper
3 cups polenta flour or cornmeal
7½ cups boiling water

Sauté the onion, carrot, celery, garlic, and herbs in the olive oil in a large pan until the onion is transparent. Pour in the tomato sauce, add the sausages, and season with salt and pepper. Cover and simmer for about 1½ hours.

After the first hour, pour the flour into the boiling water in a large pan in a steady stream. Stir constantly and cook at a slow boil for about 30 minutes. The polenta is cooked when it comes away from the sides of the pan.

Pour the polenta in the center of a clean table or work surface. Spread it out sideways a little, then pour the sausage mixture on top and spread that around a little. Now hand forks so that everyone can eat what is in the center of the table.

POLENTA PASTISSADA

LASAGNE-STYLE POLENTA

Polenta is a staple in northern Italy, where it is as popular as pasta is in the south. The basic method of cooking it is below. Many households keep cold, cooked polenta ready for frying or turning into other dishes.

This old traditional country dish from the Veneto makes a wonderful golden cake. Polenta is cut into slices, then arranged in layers with a tomato and veal sauce, cheese, and butter and baked like lasagne.

SERVES 8

2¼ cups polenta flour or cornmeal
3¾ cups boiling water

SAUCE

6 oz (about ¾ cup) dried porcini or
other dried mushrooms (ceps)
1 onion, chopped
1 carrot, chopped
1 stick celery, chopped
10 tablespoons butter
5 oz veal steak, trimmed and cubed
⅓ cup dry white wine
½ lb fresh ripe tomatoes, peeled, seeded
and chopped
½ teaspoon tomato paste
salt and pepper
2½ oz piece of Parmesan cheese
¼ cup chicken livers, cleaned, and chopped

KITCHEN UTENSILS *Natural materials such as wood, copper, and cast-iron are favored in the country kitchen.*

In a large saucepan add the polenta flour to the boiling water and stir quickly to a smooth texture. Cook for 30 minutes, stirring almost constantly until the polenta comes away from the side of the pan. Pour it out onto a board and let it set slightly. When it is cool and solid, slice it into ¾-inch thick strips.

Cover the dried mushrooms with lukewarm water and leave to soak for about 15 minutes.

Meanwhile, put the chopped onion, carrot, and celery in a skillet with about one-third of the butter and fry over low heat until soft. Add the meat and cook briefly on all sides. Pour in the wine and boil rapidly for about 5 minutes to evaporate the alcohol. Add the tomatoes and tomato paste, and season and stir. Cover and simmer for 30 minutes.

Drain the mushrooms, chop if large and stir them into the skillet. Cook for another 30 minutes. Cut the Parmesan cheese into flakes. Cook the chicken livers quickly in about 2 tablespoons of the butter.

Butter an ovenproof dish large enough to take the slices of polenta and the meat and tomato sauce. Arrange a layer of polenta slices on the bottom, pour a little sauce over and scatter a few flakes of cheese over it. Cover with another layer of polenta slices, dot with butter and a few chicken livers and more flaked Parmesan.

Continue in this way with alternate layers — meat and tomato sauce and Parmesan or chicken livers, butter, and Parmesan, ending with Parmesan and butter. Bake in a 400°F oven for 20−25 minutes. Serve at once with a full-bodied red wine.

POLENTA DI PATATE

POTATO POLENTA

This is an unusual recipe because the polenta is not cooked, simply combined with cooked, mashed potato. In a peasant community 7 lb of potatoes would probably be needed to serve eight and the sauce would be less generous.

SERVES 5–6

3½ lb Irish potatoes
salt and pepper
4 tablespoons polenta flour (or cornmeal)
large onion, finely sliced
2 tablespoons butter
2 tablespoons cooking oil
10 oz slab bacon, cubed
about 10 oz piece mozzarella, Swiss, or stracchino
cheese, cut into cubes
olive oil and lemon juice for tossing

Cook the potatoes in salted boiling water until soft. Mash them with a solid potato masher, preferably in a copper bowl, certainly in a metal one (the perfect tool for this job is an Irish masher – rather like a culinary shillelagh!).

When they are smooth, add the polenta flour a little at a time, and keep mashing until the potato comes away from the sides with no difficulty. This procedure should take about 30 minutes. To keep the potato polenta hot, either hold the metal bowl over a very low heat or mash off the heat and keep returning to the heat every few minutes to reheat. The first option is better if you can manage it.

In a separate pan, sauté the onions with the butter and oil until golden, then add the bacon and fry until crisp. When the polenta is smooth and very hot, add the cheese cubes and the sautéed ingredients to the metal bowl and mix thoroughly. Tip the whole thing out onto a big wooden board and smooth over.

To serve, using a long piece of thick, clean white thread, cut through the polenta cake like cutting through cheese with a wire. Cut into big chunks, put a chunk on each plate, and serve with a bowl of pickles and cooked beans tossed lightly in olive oil and lemon juice.

CANEDERLI DI FEGATO

LIVER DUMPLINGS

Strictly this is not a pasta dish, but any Italian would understand its being included here, for it is cooked and served "in brodo," like so many stuffed pastas. A rosé wine is the traditional drink to serve with these dumplings. I suggest the delightful Casteller from the vineyards of the Trentino in the north, where this dish is enjoyed.

SERVES 6

16 slices stale white bread, 2 or 3 days old
14 oz calf's liver or chicken livers
a handful of fresh parsley leaves, finely chopped
1 stick celery, finely chopped
1 small onion, finely chopped
a sprig of fresh marjoram, finely chopped
salt and pepper
a pinch of grated nutmeg
grated peel of 1 lemon
1 tablespoon olive oil
2 large eggs
5½ cups cake flour
7–8 tablespoons milk
6 cups good meat or vegetable stock

DRYING MAIZE *Dried maize, once a part of farmhouse cooking, is now mainly used as chickenfeed. Corn-fed chicken tastes especially good!*

Cut the bread into thin slices, then cube it. Mince the liver to a pulp. Mix together the vegetables, herbs, bread, and liver. Season with salt, pepper, and nutmeg then add the lemon peel, olive oil, and eggs and stir thoroughly. Add the flour and the milk and stir vigorously until you have a thick, smooth mass.

Bring a large pan of water to a boil. Shape the dough into balls about the size of a baby's fist, slide them into the water, and cook gently for 20 minutes.

Meanwhile, heat the stock. When the dumplings are ready, ladle the stock into 6 bowls. Scoop out the dumplings from the water with a slotted spoon and divide them equally between the 6 bowls. Serve at once with a sprinkling of extra parsley and marjoram, and more stock if you like.

GRANO AL RAGU

CORN GRAIN WITH MEAT AND TOMATO SAUCE

This was originally a cheap peasant dish, made from dried maize. The maize was soaked for 12 hours then cooked in fresh water for 3–4 more, until soft, then served with sauce. The meat from the sauce can be served separately as a second course with a green vegetable or salad.

SERVES 6

6–8 ears of corn, or 2½ lb frozen or canned, drained corn kernels
¼ cup chopped fresh parsley leaves
2 cloves garlic
large pinch chili powder
large pinch grated nutmeg
1¾ oz (¼ cup) pecorino or Parmesan cheese
1¼ lb pork steak, in one slice
3 slices fatty bacon
2 tablespoons olive oil
1 tablespoon pork drippings or shortening
⅓ cup red or white wine
1 lb canned tomatoes, seeded
salt and pepper

Mix the parsley and garlic together, then mix in the chili and nutmeg. Chop a little over half the pecorino into tiny cubes and add them too. Beat the pork to flatten as much as possible, then spread the parsley mixture over it. Cover with the bacon, roll it up on itself like a jelly roll and tie securely with strong string.

Choose a small flameproof casserole or saucepan into which the meat fits neatly. Heat the oil and drippings and brown the meat on all sides, then add the wine. Cook for 5 minutes, then add the tomatoes, and season with salt and pepper. Cover and simmer for about 2 hours, stirring the tomato occasionally and adding water if it appears to be drying out.

If you're using fresh corn, boil for about 10–12 minutes. When tender, remove the kernels from the cob, drain and moisten with the sauce from the casserole. Serve with a small slice of meat – though originally this would have been part of another course. Scatter with plenty of grated pecorino or Parmesan cheese.

MEAT, POULTRY, GAME, SALUMI

Meat, always a delicacy in the farmhouse kitchen, is made the most of in special festive dishes and, more sparingly used, provides the base for delicious everyday casseroles and stews.

STUFATO DI MANZO CON PATATE *(p 61)*

TORTINO
DI PATATE E CARNE

MEAT AND POTATO CAKE

Originally from Austria, where it is called G'rostl, this dish is a very simple and economical way of using up leftover boiled beef to make a delicious fried "cake" of meat and potatoes flavored with chives.

SERVES 4

4 tablespoons butter
2 tablespoons chopped fresh chives
1 lb cold boiled beef, cut into small chunks
*4 cold boiled medium-sized potatoes, cut
into small chunks*
salt and pepper

Heat the butter in a 7-inch skillet and snip the chives into the butter. Add the meat, potatoes, and salt and pepper. Mix together very thoroughly, then cook for 10 minutes, pressing down with a metal spatula to create a crisp crust underneath.

Turn the potato cake over by sliding it on to a plate and then tipping it back into the hot pan. Cook until the other side is also just crisp, then serve at once. It is also very good cold and makes an excellent item for a picnic.

STRACOTTO

POT-ROASTED BEEF

This delicious, juicy, and tender pot-roasted beef is an ancient dish which goes back several centuries in Italian peasant cookery. Originally the pot used to make it in would have been made of glazed terracotta with a tight-fitting lid. In those days no other flavoring ingredients were added; the dish was simply the best quality stewing beef cooked in red wine.

SERVES 6

*3 lb stewing beef in one piece, rolled
and tied*
4 cloves garlic, cut lengthwise into strips
2 tablespoons pork dripping, or shortening
1 onion, chopped
1 carrot, chopped
1 stick celery, chopped
6 tablespoons butter
*1 tablespoon tomato paste diluted in about
1½ cups stock, plus extra stock if required*
salt and pepper

Pierce the meat with a skewer and insert slivers of garlic into the holes. Mix the dripping with the chopped vegetables, then put this mixture into a deep, heavy flameproof casserole into which the meat fits. Add the butter and sauté the vegetables for 5 minutes. Then add the meat and cook it on all sides.

Pour in the stock mixture and season with salt and pepper. Cover with a tight lid and cook very slowly for 5 or 6 hours, basting the meat occasionally with more stock and turning it over.

At the end of the cooking time, remove the meat from the sauce. Slice it thickly and arrange on a serving dish, pour over the sauce from the pot, and serve at once.

COWS DRINKING AT MARKET-PLACE *A martyred St. Sebastian presides over this peaceful scene in the village of Glorenza near the Austrian Border.*

LESSO RIFATTO ALLA SENESE

BOILED BEEF IN THE SIENNA STYLE

This excellent and typically frugal dish uses up all the odd bits of meat leftover from making the ever-present Italian meat stock. Their flavor is normally rather boring and unimaginative when eaten on their own. It also works very well with the leftovers of a roast, provided that it is fairly plain and unflavored. In itself it is not very substantial, but it is one of those Tuscan dishes that marries perfectly with the local bean dishes such as Fagioli Stufati (see page 101).

SERVES 4

1 lb boiled beef, brisket or roast beef
¼ cup olive oil
1 large onion, finely sliced
¾ lb fresh ripe tomatoes, seeded and coarsely chopped
½ teaspoon tomato paste
salt and pepper
chopped fresh basil or dried basil, to taste

Slice the meat into thick rounds. Heat the oil in a saucepan, add the onions, and gently fry until golden but soft. Add meat, tomatoes, and tomato paste and season.

Sprinkle the basil over the top and cook through until hot and bubbling. Arrange the meat on a serving platter, pour the sauce over it, and serve at once.

CECI CON LA ZAMPINA DI MAIALE

CHICK PEAS WITH PIG'S FEET

The original version of the dish called for tempia di maiale (above the eyes) which is the fattiest part of the pig, and the result was an extremely heavy, greasy dish. The idea behind dishes like this was to provide internal central heating for peasants living in icy-cold conditions. In this updated version the feet are used instead, making a more tasty and nourishing dish. The timing is for modern chick peas too.

SERVES 6–8

¾ cup dried chick peas
a pinch baking soda
2 pig's feet, split and washed
2 lb pork loin, cubed in big chunks
1 large carrot, cut into cubes
2 large sticks celery, cut into sections
3 small onions, peeled and quartered
a sprig of fresh rosemary
a sprig of fresh sage
salt and pepper
pickled peppers
pickled gherkins
pickled onions
Parmesan cheese, freshly grated, to serve

Cover the chick peas with cold water, add the baking soda and soak for 24 hours. Drain and wash in cold water. Put the feet, meat, vegetables and herbs in a large casserole, cover with water. Add salt and pepper and simmer slowly for 4 hours until the meat is falling off the feet and the fat has almost turned to jelly.

About 1½ hours before the feet will be ready, cover the chick peas with plenty of fresh water and boil slowly, without salt, over a low heat without removing the lid.

Add the chick peas to the meat and vegetables and cook for a further 30 minutes, then serve. The meat is usually taken out and served with pickles, while the remaining mixture is served as a very thick soup, sprinkled with grated Parmesan cheese.

FASUI CUL MUSET

BEANS WITH COTECHINO SAUSAGE

Cotechino, called Muset in Friuli dialect, is a deliciously spicy, rich and soft sausage, traditionally served on New Year's Eve with lentils. In the Friuli, it is eaten throughout the winter months and often cooked with beans, onion, and butter in this delectable, simple recipe. Cotechino sausage is available at good Italian delicatessens; see the package for cooking instructions.

SERVES 4

1 cup dried beans (any variety you prefer)
1 large Spanish onion or 2 smaller ones, finely sliced
4 tablespoons butter
3 tablespoons light olive oil
6 fresh sage leaves, chopped
salt and pepper
1 cotechino sausage

Soak the beans overnight in cold water, drain, and wash them. Cover with clean cold water and boil very fast for 10 minutes, drain, and return to the saucepan. Cover with fresh water and simmer slowly without a lid.

Sauté the onion in the butter and oil in a skillet until the onion is crisp and golden. Pour the onion and the fat into the beans and stir, sprinkle in the sage, and season to taste. Continue to cook for 1½–2 hours, until tender, depending on the size of the beans.

Cook the cotechino separately according to the instructions on the package, then slice it into thick rounds. Add the sliced sausage to the beans and heat through for 5 minutes. Serve on warm plates with plenty of robust red wine, such as a Merlot or Cabernet.

COPPA SENESE

FRESH SIENNESE SALUME

This is a preserved meat – a salume – but one for immediate consumption; it isn't one you can hang up and use over several months. To cook the sausage properly, you will need to make yourself a sausage bag about 8–10 inches long and 3–4 inches wide out of doubled muslin or a piece of cotton sheet to hold the sausage ingredients in shape.

SERVES ABOUT 10

*the ears, head, feet, tail and trimming of skin
from a freshly butchered pig
2 tablespoons salt per 2 lb raw pig
¾ teaspoon ground black pepper per 2 lb raw pig
4 cloves garlic, finely chopped
grated peel of 1 orange
grated peel of 1 lemon
½ teaspoon mixed spices
½ teaspoon ground cinnamon
1 teaspoon fennel or caraway seeds*

Trim and clean all the parts of the pig. Singe the hairy areas over an open flame, then scrape off the hairs and hard skin with a sharp knife. Wash the pieces very carefully, then weigh them together and make a note of the weight.

Bring a large pan of water to a boil, then immerse all the pieces of pig in the water. Bring back to a boil, then turn off the heat. Leave the pan undisturbed until the following day.

The next day, pour off the water and replace with fresh water, bring back to a boil, and simmer for about 3 hours. Remove from the heat and pick off all the meat and fat, discarding all the bones.

Chop all the meat coarsely, put it all into a bowl, and add the salt and pepper according to the raw weight. Mix in the garlic, grated orange and lemon peel, the spices, and the seeds. Stir together very thoroughly, then spoon it all into a cloth bag. Tie it up firmly with string and hang it up to dry in a cool, airy place away from pets and insects for 24–48 hours until firm and dry.

Remove the bag and slice the meat into rounds. Serve with plenty of bread and wine as a snack or antipasto and eat within 3 days.

ANIMELLE AL PROSCIUTTO

SWEETBREADS WITH HAM

This robust variety meat dish is typical of the provincial areas around Rome. It is traditionally served with fresh peas or artichokes with melted butter and plenty of parsley, which adds a welcome touch of color.

SERVES 4

*1¼ lb lambs' sweetbreads
salt
2½ oz prosciutto crudo, or other Parma ham,
coarsely chopped
1 onion, finely sliced
1 tablespoon olive oil or 1 tablespoon butter
5 tablespoons good broth
2 tablespoons butter
½ tablespoon all-purpose flour
freshly ground black pepper*

Carefully peel the membrane from the sweetbreads, cover with cold water and leave to soak for 3 hours. This will ensure they remain perfectly white. Drain and toss into boiling water for 3 minutes. Drain again and rinse under cold water, then pat dry and slice into neat rounds.

Fry the prosciutto and onion in the olive oil or butter in a saucepan for 5 or 6 minutes. Add the sweetbreads and reduce the heat to as low as possible. Fry them very carefully, turning them once, for a total of 10–12 minutes. Add about 3 tablespoons of the stock as they cook.

Remove the sweetbreads and arrange them on a warm dish. Mash the 2 tablespoons butter and the flour, together and stir into the pan juices, with the remaining stock. Season with pepper. Stir together and cook to a smooth sauce. Pour the sauce over the sweetbreads and serve at once, with a green vegetable to garnish.

VINEYARDS IN AUTUMN *(p 72) Italian vines grow vertically up poles, not horizontally as in France. In the autumn, the vine leaves turn a spectacular red-gold.*

TRIPPA DI MONGANA ALLA CANEPINA

VEAL TRIPE COOKED IN THE CANEPINA STYLE

SERVES 4–6

2 lb calf's honeycomb tripe (or lamb's tripe)
1 onion, finely chopped
2 cloves garlic, finely chopped
1 large carrot, finely chopped
1 stick celery, finely chopped
a large pinch of dried marjoram
peel of 1 lemon, finely chopped
3 strips skinned boneless fresh bacon, cubed
1 ham bone
1 tablespoon tomato paste
salt
country-style bread
Parmesan cheese, freshly grated, to serve

The most important ingredient of this traditional winter dish from the Marche is the ham bone, which imparts a delicious flavor. It is a dish from the province of Ancona and varies slightly from one village to another. The final result is a rich, rib-sticking concoction which is served with big slabs of coarse country-style bread, lightly toasted, in the oven, then sprinkled with olive oil. The best kind of tripe is calf's, although lamb's tripe can be substituted.

Wash the tripe in several waters, trimming off loose pieces. Scald it by pouring boiling water over it. Put it in a saucepan, cover with cold water, bring to a boil, and cook for about 20 minutes. Drain, wash again and cube.

In a deep, heavy-bottomed pan, put the chopped onion, garlic, carrot, celery, dried marjoram, lemon peel, and cubed pork and fry together slowly until the vegetables are soft. Add the tripe and the ham bone and cover with water. Stir in the tomato paste and salt to taste and simmer for 2 hours, adding more water as required. Serve with plenty of bread and grated Parmesan cheese.

FARMHOUSE *Thrift is the farmer's watchword — he won't be too bothered by his flaking stucco walls until the rainy months come around again.*

POLLO ALLA TOSCANA

TUSCAN-STYLE COUNTRY CHICKEN

A deliciously simple and very typically Tuscan chicken casserole. Serve with mashed potatoes and a green vegetable and more white wine.

SERVES 4

1 cup dried porcini mushrooms (ceps)
1½ cups warm chicken stock
3¼ lb chicken, preferably corn fed,
cut into 8 pieces
6 tablespoons unsalted butter
⅓ cup olive oil
⅔ cup dry white wine
salt and pepper
1 cup tomato sauce
1 tablespoon all-purpose flour

Wash and pick over the mushrooms carefully. Cover with half the stock and leave to soak for about 15 minutes.

Heat 2 tablespoons of the butter with the oil in a flameproof casserole. Add the chicken pieces and brown them all over. Add the wine and season with salt and pepper. Cook for 5 minutes to evaporate the alcohol, then add the tomato sauce. Stir in the rest of the stock and the mushrooms. Cover and cook over a low heat for 40 minutes.

Remove the chicken from the pot and keep warm. Mash the remaining butter with the flour and mix it into the liquid in the casserole. Cook until the sauce is thick and smooth, then pour it over the chicken and serve at once.

POLLO RIPIENO ALLE NOCI

STUFFED CHICKEN WITH WALNUTS

From the mountains of Trentino comes this delicate boiled boned chicken with its delicious stuffing of walnuts, nutmeg, and pine nuts.

SERVES 6

3½ lb chicken, boned
2 stale white bread rolls, all crust removed
milk
½ cup shelled fresh walnuts
¼ cup pine nuts
5 oz marrow from beef shin bones
the giblets from the chicken
salt and pepper
1 heaping tablespoon Parmesan cheese
¼ teaspoon nutmeg, grated
1 or 2 large eggs, beaten

Bone the chicken by slitting the skin along the backbone and then working a sharp knife between the flesh and the carcass. Remove all the bones you can see, scraping the flesh off them and always working from the inside. Your butcher can do this for you.

Cover the bread with milk and leave to soak for about 15 minutes. Meanwhile, blanch the walnuts in boiling water and remove the skins. Put them in a blender or food processor and grind them; a food processor makes a coarser mix. Cook the giblets in boiling water for 5–6 minutes, then remove the neck bone and process the flesh to a fine pulp with the beef marrow. Remove the bread from the milk and squeeze it dry in your hand. Process the bread with the giblets. Mix in the ground nuts, pine nuts, and nutmeg, seasoning to taste with salt and pepper. Stir in a little egg spoonful by spoonful, adding more if the mixture feels at all dry.

Put the mixture inside the boned chicken and sew it up along the back with strong string or thread. Put the chicken in a large saucepan, cover with water, cover and simmer over a medium heat for about 1 hour. Serve hot or cold, carved across in slices.

UNSHACKLED CART BY AN OLD STONE WALL *The chicken pecking around the old wooden cart looks ready to stand in for the usual team of oxen.*

CONIGLIO A SUCCITTU

STEWED SARDINIAN RABBIT

This deliciously vinegary rabbit stew is often served cold – in fact many Sardinians claim it is much better cooked and eaten cold the following day. It is also an excellent way to cook hare or venison.

SERVES 6

3 lb rabbit, cut in pieces
1 rabbit's liver
¼ cup olive oil
1 large onion, finely chopped
4 cloves garlic, chopped
½ cup capers, washed and dried and
finely chopped
salt
5 tablespoons water
5 tablespoons wine vinegar

Wash and dry the rabbit. Chop the trimmed liver. Heat the oil in a heavy-bottomed skillet, add the rabbit pieces and cook until browned all over.

Mix the chopped liver, onion, and garlic together with half the capers and stir into the pan. Cook over medium heat for 20 minutes, then season with salt. Add the wine vinegar with about ¼ cup water and pour over the meat. Add the remaining capers, cover, and cook gently until tender, up to 45 minutes, checking that it is not burning. Serve hot or cold.

77

TORESANI ALLO SPIEDO

PIGEONS WITH JUNIPER BERRIES

Toresani is the Venetian word used to describe a particular variety of pigeon, also called Torraioli. I have found this dish works with any type of pigeon and that the essential part of the dish is that you must cook on a spit, either in the oven or outside over a barbecue or open fire.

SERVES 4

10 juniper berries
2 bay leaves
salt and pepper
4 tablespoons olive oil
1 rosemary branch, about 6 inches long
4 small, plump, gutted and cleaned pigeons
4 oz fresh pork fat (skinned and removed from
the back in a sheet)

Crush the juniper berries in a mortar along with the bay leaves and some salt and pepper. Add the olive oil and mix together.

Dip the rosemary branch in the flavored oil and paint the inside of each bird with the oil. Cut the fat into 4 strips and wrap a strip around each bird. Secure it in place with string, then thread each bird on to the spit and cook over medium heat for 30 minutes, basting with the remaining oil.

Just before serving remove the string around the fat. Traditionally, this is a dish served with polenta (page 55) that has been sliced and fried quickly in a pan with a little olive oil until brown on both sides.

TORESANI ALLO SPIEDO

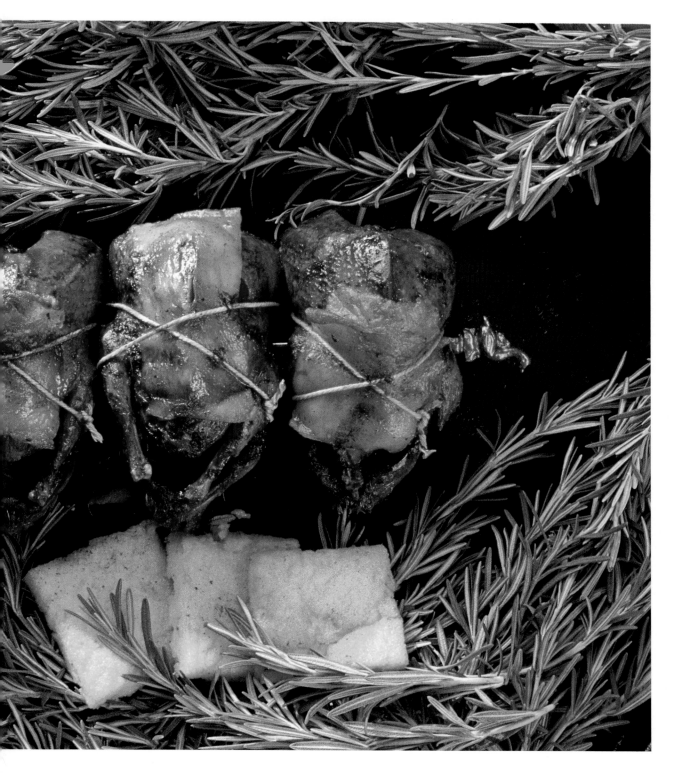

BURRIDA DI PESCE FRESCO

LIGURIAN FISH STEW

In this tasty fish stew from the seaside region of Liguria, all the flavors of the sea are blended together with fresh tomatoes, herbs, and wine to make a truly memorable dish.

SERVES 6

2½ lb mixed fresh fish, including a variety such as dab or flounder fillets, halibut, kingfish, sculpin, angler (monkfish) and rockfish or striped bass
1 lb mixed shellfish, such as shrimp, scampi, and crayfish, shelled
2 lb onions, sliced
1 lb fresh tomatoes, peeled, seeded, and chopped
½ teaspoon tomato paste
2 tablespoons dried oregano
a handful of fresh parsley, chopped
⅔ cup dry white wine
olive oil
salt and pepper

Wash and trim all the fish and shellfish. Grease a flameproof casserole large enough to take all the ingredients. Scatter a layer of sliced onions on the bottom. Cover with a layer of fish and shellfish. Season with salt and pepper then cover with some of the chopped tomato.

Repeat the layering with onions, a little oil, then fish and shellfish, and finally tomatoes and the paste. Sprinkle the herbs over the top. Pour in the wine very carefully, then dribble olive oil over the top. Cook, uncovered, over a very low heat for about 35 minutes or until the liquid in the casserole has thickened to a soupy consistency. Serve hot or just tepid with plenty of crusty bread.

ANGUILLA ALLA NUORESE

NUORO-STYLE EEL

Eel is an acquired taste for many people, but cooked properly it can be really delicious and loses much of its muddy aftertaste. This recipe comes from Nuoro in Sardinia. The fish can be skinned before use or not, but the fins must be removed.

SERVES 4

2 tablespoons olive oil
2 lb eel, cut into chunks
3 cloves garlic, peeled, and chopped
2 lb ripe fresh tomatoes, peeled,
seeded, and chopped
½ teaspoon tomato paste
salt and pepper
a handful of fresh parsley leaves, chopped
a handful of fresh basil leaves, chopped

Skin the eel if there is a fat layer beneath the skin, and cut it into chunks. Heat the oil in a heavy-bottomed skillet, add the eel chunks and brown them on all sides, then remove from the oil and set aside.

Put the garlic into the oil and sauté for 2 minutes, then add the tomatoes and paste, stir together, and season. Cook for about 10 minutes, then return the eel to the skillet. Cover and cook for 5 – 8 minutes, depending on the thickness of the eel. Uncover, scatter the herbs over and serve straight from the skillet.

LUCCIO IN STUFATO

STEWED PIKE

Pike is one of those awkward fish that are difficult to cook as their flavor and texture are somewhat limiting. In the lakes of Lombardy they are plentiful and are cooked in this flavorful stew with red wine and vegetables. The recipe works with any rich, meaty fish – tuna is ideal, and does not have the awkward little bones of a pike.

SERVES 4

1 pike, gutted, about 1¼ lb
4 tablespoons butter
3 tablespoons olive oil
1⅓ cups onions, chopped
1⅓ cups young tender carrots sliced in rounds
2 large sticks celery, finely chopped
all-purpose flour
¾ cup robust red wine
salt and pepper
1 cup cold water

Wash the fish and remove as many scales as possible drawing a knife down it. Leave to drain.

Heat the butter and oil in a flameproof casserole, add the vegetables and fry gently until soft. Coat the fish with flour, add to the vegetables, and fry quickly to seal on both sides. Pour over the wine and season thoroughly. Cook over high heat for 5 minutes to evaporate the alcohol, then add the water. Cover and cook over a gentle heat for 1 hour. Carefully remove the fish and lay it on a warm platter. In a food processor or food mill, puree the vegetables in the casserole and pour the resulting smooth sauce over the fish. Serve at once.

SARDINIAN BOATMAN *A Sardinian peasant punts a boat laden with reeds across the tranquil waters.*

RIFUGI AND ALLOTMENT (p 92) *These whitewashed cabins provide shelter for the days when farming is far from home. They are set in a cultivated plot with vegetables and fruit trees.*

TROTELLE AL POMODORO

TROUT IN TOMATO SAUCE

Wonderfully fresh and tender young trout, simmered in a fresh tomato sauce laced with olive oil, parsley, and garlic make up this fine dish from the mountains of the Abruzzi and the Molise. Do not use large trout.

SERVES 4

⅓ cup fresh parsley, chopped
1 clove garlic, chopped
⅓ cup olive oil
1 lb ripe fresh tomatoes, peeled, seeded,
and chopped
⅓ teaspoon tomato paste
salt and pepper
4 small trout, total weight about 1¾ lb
gutted and cleaned

Put the parsley, garlic, and olive oil in a pan large enough to take all the fish, then fry for 1–2 minutes. Add the tomatoes and paste and mix together. Season with salt and pepper, then simmer for about 5 minutes.

Place the trout in the tomato mixture and spoon it over them so they are semi-covered. Cover and cook for about 20 minutes, then serve with a dry fresh white wine like Frascati.

BORETO ALLA GRAISANA

GRADO-STYLE TURBOT

Always accompanied by the soft and creamy white polenta which is eaten locally, this superbly simple dish allows the fine flavor of the fish to shine through.

SERVES 3–4

⅓ cup olive oil
3 whole cloves garlic
1 lb turbot, cleaned, in one piece
salt and pepper
good quality wine vinegar

Heat the oil in a saucepan large enough to take the fish. Add the garlic and fry until dark brown. Remove the garlic and lay the fish in the hot oil. Sprinkle with salt and pepper and a little vinegar. Cook for 5 minutes, spooning the hot oil over the fish.

Pour in enough water to come halfway up the fish. Continue cooking for 10–12 minutes or until the fish is cooked through. Serve hot with polenta.

MUGGINE AL SALE

MULLET BAKED IN SALT

Any large fish with a thick scaly skin such as porgy will work perfectly in this recipe, but it must be freshly caught and fairly big — over 2¼ lb at least. It can serve up to ten people depending on the size of the fish. Don't be put off by the distinct lack of other ingredients: fish cooked like this will taste of the sea and of the fish — nothing else will come between it and you!

SERVES 4

2¼ lb ungutted, unscaled mullet, dorade
or other large scaly fish
rock salt

Wash the fish but do not cut it or touch it in any other way. Cover the bottom of an ovenproof dish large enough to take the fish comfortably with a 3-inch layer of rock salt.

Place the ungutted fish on the top and cover it completely with more salt to a depth of 3 inches. Press down hard on the salt with the heel of your hands so as to create a compact cover.

Cook in a 375°F oven for 1 hour, then crack the salt crust and remove salt and skin in one go to reveal a fragrant fish. Serve at once. You can remove the salt at the table as an added attraction, if you like.

CUSCUSU

SICILIAN COUSCOUS

The Arab dish of couscous is very popular in eastern Sicily where housewives prepare it regularly and therefore have all the correct equipment. They start by making the couscous itself, which is then steamed and served with a delicious fish stew, which is also called couscous. You can buy dried North African couscous ready-made and this will need the same long cooking time. If you use 2¼ lb instant couscous, soak it for 10 minutes in boiling fish broth, then fork it, to separate the grains. Or serve the fish couscous with rice. In all these cases I would compensate by adding the saffron to the fish stew.

SERVES 6

HOME-MADE COUSCOUS
1 cup fine grain semolina
1 cup thick grain semolina
½ teaspoon powdered saffron
½ cup hot water
¼ cup olive oil
1 tablespoon ground black pepper
a large pinch of ground cinnamon
a large pinch of grated nutmeg
fish stock or water, to steam

FISH STEW
2 cloves garlic, chopped
½ cup olive oil
a handful of fresh parsley leaves, chopped
1 large onion, sliced
1 bay leaf
3 canned tomatoes, seeded, and chopped
2½ lb assorted fish such as mackerel, cod, or pollock, and
eel, cleaned and gutted
salt and pepper

OLD HOUSE AT A QUAYSIDE *This old house with its Arab-style windows could easily date back to medieval times.*

Mix the semolinas together very thoroughly. Dissolve the saffron in hot water, then put 1 tablespoonful of the diluted saffron into a large wide bowl with a handful of semolina. Rub the semolinas up the sides and across the bottom of the bowl, making it granular (pieces no bigger than a peppercorn), then scoop out the couscous and spread on a clean tablecloth.

Go through all the semolina this way, a small amount at a time with a little bright yellow saffron water. Leave it spread out like this to dry out.

Pour the stock or water into a saucepan and put a large metal colander on top. Wrap a cloth around the colander where it meets the top of the pot so as not to lose any of the steam in the next stage of cooking.

Pour the granular couscous into the colander and pour the olive oil over it. Mix together with your hands and then lay a heavy clean cloth on top of the grains and a lid on top of that. Bring the liquid to a boil and let it boil very slowly, for 1½ hours so the couscous cooks in the steam coming through the holes of the colander.

After about 1 hour, start the fish stew. Sauté the garlic and the oil in a large saucepan or flameproof casserole with the parsley and onion for about 3 minutes, then add the bay leaf and tomatoes. Cook for about 5–6 minutes, then add all the fish and season with salt and pepper. Add about 9 cups of water, enough to cover the fish, then cover with a lid and simmer for about 25 minutes.

When the couscous is ready, pour it into a bowl, sprinkle about 5 tablespoons of the liquid used for steaming over the grains and stir them well to separate them. Cover with a lid, wrap the bowl up in a woolen cloth or towel, and put it in a warm place to swell. Overall it will need about 1 hour to swell.

When the fish is ready, scoop out the pieces with a slotted spoon and keep in a warm place. Pour the fish stock through a strainer – there should be about 2¼ cups. Pour half of this into another jug and let it cool a little, so that it thickens to make the final sauce. Meanwhile, the couscous needs sprinkling with as much fish broth as it will absorb every 15 minutes, and stirring each time to make sure the grains are not sticking together. Keep it warm all the time.

After an hour, sprinkle the couscous with the pepper, cinnamon, and nutmeg and moisten with a little of the reserved fish stock. Arrange the hot fish on top and serve at once.

CIME DI RAPE STUFATE

STEWED TURNIP TOPS

SERVES 4

4 lb turnip tops or spinach
salt and pepper
2 cloves garlic
3 bay leaves
⅓ cup olive oil
⅔ cup rosé wine

Nothing is ever wasted in a peasant household, whatever is not eaten by the family will be used up by the animals. But this is not the case with the humble turnip top, which is so delicious it is considered too good for the animals! In Apulia they are especially fond of this vegetable and it turns up in all sorts of recipes, often accompanying pasta. This recipe uses garlic, rosé wine, and bay leaves to make a very tasty dish. If you haven't any turnip tops, try using sliced turnips or another similar green vegetable, such as spinach or beet leaves.

Wash and trim the turnip tops or spinach and then cook them in a covered pan with just the water that adheres to the leaves. As they cook, push the leaves aside and remove all the water that forms as they cook, it is bitter and would spoil the flavor. When there is no more water, add the salt and pepper, garlic cloves, bay leaves, oil, and wine. Stir and cook for a further 15 minutes.

CARCIOFI CON PATATE IN UMIDO

STEWED ARTICHOKES WITH POTATOES

This lovely Sardinian dish is one of my all time great favorites. It makes a vegetarian main course.

SERVES 4

6 globe artichokes or 12 Jerusalem artichokes, scrubbed
juice of 1 lemon
⅓ cup olive oil
2 cloves garlic, chopped
a handful of fresh parsley leaves, finely chopped
6 potatoes, peeled and cut into the same size chunks
salt and pepper

Peel off the outer leaves if using globe artichokes and trim round the base with a knife. Remove all spines that cover the base beneath the soft inner leaves and cut into 4. Drop into a bowl of cold water mixed with the lemon juice. Alternatively, peel Jerusalem artichokes, cutting them into chunks of roughly the same size, and drop them into water with lemon juice.

Heat the oil in a large pan, add the garlic and the parsley and cook for a minute. Add the artichokes and brown them all over. Add a little water, season, and cover. Cook very gently for about 30 minutes for globe artichokes, if they are large, 20 minutes for Jerusalem artichokes, adding the potatoes 20 minutes before the end. Add a little water if necessary while cooking, but the finished dish should not be watery.

LA PEPERONATA

STEWED PEPPERS

This is the quintessential Sicilian dish, although I have heard people say it comes from bizarre places like Piedmont! The erotic, pulpy, fleshy, and juicy bell pepper, be it red, green or yellow, comes first and foremost from this part of Italy where it was introduced from Latin America along with chocolate and coffee. Real bell pepper experts claim that the very best ones are from Calabria, where indeed their texture and size verge on the obscene. But the glorious island of Sicily is rich with bright vegetable dishes like this one, many of which have the flavorful green Sicilian olives added to make the dish inimitably Sicilian. If bell pepper dishes exist in Northern Italy, then it is because they have been introduced by southern immigrants going north in search of well-paid factory work — but here under the southern sun is where the peppers bring color and glitter to the poorest kitchens.

SERVES 4

4 juicy fat bell peppers
3 large onions, sliced
5 tablespoons olive oil
¾ lb fresh ripe tomatoes, seeded,
¼ teaspoon tomato paste
salt
3 tablespoons wine vinegar
½ cup green olives, pitted, and chopped

Wash the peppers, cut them in half, and remove all the seeds and the inner membranes. Cut them in half again — or in strips, if they seem very large — and set aside. Sauté the onions in the oil until just soft, then add the tomatoes and tomato paste, and the peppers. Stir and season with salt.

When the peppers are sealed all over, sprinkle in the vinegar and add the olives. Stir well, then cook until the peppers are just cooked, not mushy. Serve hot or cold, with a main course dish or on their own.

PRIEST AND PARISHIONER *(p 104) Seeking out the most perfect vegetables is as much a part of the daily round for the priest as it is for most of his congregation.*
SUNFLOWER FIELD *(p 106) Sunflower oil is a great Italian export, and the fields of flowers make a fantastic splash of color.*

MELANZANE AL FORNO

BAKED EGGPLANT

From Apulia comes this deliciously summery eggplant dish. It's got all the flavors of the south — capers, olives, pecorino cheese and of course the velvety rich, Eastern texture and taste of the wonderful eggplant.

SERVES 4

4 smallish eggplants
4 tablespoons soft bread crumbs
4 tablespoons pecorino or Parmesan cheese, grated
⅓ cup black olives, pitted and chopped
5 tablespoons olive oil
salt and pepper
a handful of fresh parsley, finely chopped
a handful of capers, washed and chopped
a handful of dried bread crumbs

Cut the eggplants in half lengthwise. Very carefully scoop out the pulp with a small spoon. Chop the pulp and prepare as in vegetable section of glossary. Mix it up with the soft bread crumbs and the cheese. Mix in the olives and fry this mixture in half the oil for 5 minutes.

Meanwhile, drop the 8 halved eggplants into a pan of boiling water and cook for 5 minutes. Stir the parsley, capers, and remaining oil into the fried mixture. Taste and season generously.

Drain and dry the halved eggplants very carefully, then spoon in the filling mixture. Arrange the filled eggplants in an oiled ovenproof dish and sprinkle the dried bread crumbs on the top. Bake in a hot 400°F oven for 20 minutes. Serve hot or cold as an excellent antipasto or as part of an all-vegetable meal.

SPINACI ALLA ROMANA

ROMAN-STYLE SPINACH

In the Lazio, they grow the widest variety of vegetables anywhere in the country. La Campagna Romana has been Rome's market garden for many centuries. Their spinach is especially sweet in this delectable and unusual recipe.

SERVES 4

⅓ cup golden raisins
2 lb fresh spinach
4 tablespoons unsalted butter
2 tablespoons olive oil
1 clove garlic, crushed
⅓ cup pine nuts
salt

Soak the raisins in warm water for 15 minutes, then drain. Meanwhile, wash the spinach very carefully, trim and cook it without liquid in a covered pan until soft. Leave it to cool, then squeeze it dry with your hands.

ITALIAN STREET MARKET *Real concentration can be read on the faces of these shoppers as they pursue the best and freshest buy in the market.*

Melt the butter in a pan with the oil, add the garlic, and fry it until crisp, then discard the garlic. Add the pine nuts and toss until brown then remove. Add the dry spinach and the raisins to the pan, tossing the spinach with 2 forks to cover it with the butter and oil. Stir in the pine nuts and salt to taste. Heat through, tossing with the forks, for 5 – 10 minutes, then serve at once.

COSTE AL POMODORO

SWISS CHARD WITH TOMATO

Swiss chard is a very popular vegetable throughout Italy but particularly in the provinces around Rome. Swiss chard has an unmistakable flavor and texture and is very easy to grow. It also is one of those vegetables which is attractive enough to grow as an ornamental edible in a border. If you really cannot get hold of chard, large romaine lettuce leaves are the closest possible alternative.

SERVES 4

1¾ lb Swiss chard or large dark green romaine lettuce leaves
¼ cup olive oil
2 cloves garlic, slightly crushed
3 salted anchovies, or 6 anchovy fillets canned in oil
6 canned tomatoes, seeded
salt and pepper

Pull the dark green chard leaves off their heavy white stalks and put the leaves in a pan with plenty of boiling water. Cook for about 8 minutes. Alternatively, blanch the romaine leaves. Drain and dry, then chop very coarsely into wide strips.

Heat the oil in a large pan, add the garlic, and fry until the garlic is brown, then discard it. Add the anchovies and the tomatoes. Mix and mash these ingredients into the oil, stirring it all together, then add the chard or lettuce. Turn it over in the sauce and season with salt and pepper. Heat through for 5 – 10 minutes, then serve hot.

MOTORBIKE WITH VEGETABLES *This useful little machine is a more industrious version of the Vespa (wasp) and is known as an Ape (bee). It is ideally suited to transporting produce from smaller farms.*

VERZOLINI DELLA VIGILIA

CHRISTMAS EVE CABBAGE

A very different Christmas specialty for the night before Christmas when it's traditional not to eat meat in Italy. It is a rustic, simple, and tasty dish, consisting of stuffed cabbage leaves stewed in tomato sauce, from the province of Parma. Serve 4–5 each as a starter.

MAKES 2 DOZEN STUFFED CABBAGE LEAVES

*1¼ lb tender small leaves from a
large cabbage
2½ slices stale white bread
6 tablespoons milk
1½ cups Parmesan cheese, freshly grated
3 large eggs, beaten
1 cup dry bread crumbs
salt and pepper
3 tablespoons olive oil
2 tablespoons butter
1 onion, finely chopped
8 canned tomatoes, sieved
1 tablespoon tomato paste
stock*

Soak the stale bread in the milk for about 10 minutes. Wash the cabbage leaves. Bring a pan of water to a boil and cook the cabbage leaves for about 8 minutes, then drain them and lay them out flat on a worktop. Choose the 2 dozen best leaves and chop the rest finely.

Squeeze the bread dry, mix with the Parmesan cheese, eggs, dry bread crumbs, and season generously. Stir in the chopped cabbage.

Spoon a little of the mixture onto each of the cabbage leaves. Fold in the sides and roll up to make a parcel, then secure it with fine string or thread.

Heat half the oil and butter in a pan and fry the parcels to seal them on all sides. Remove from the pan and set aside. Using the remaining oil and butter, sauté the onion until transparent, then add the sieved tomatoes and the paste. Stir and cook for about 15 minutes until thick and enriched, adding a little stock if necessary.

Lay the fried parcels in the sauce and cover. Cook slowly for 1 hour, adding stock if the sauce starts to dry out. Remove the string before serving piping hot.

POMODORI RIPIENI ALL'UMBRA

STUFFED TOMATOES IN THE UMBRIAN STYLE

To make this dish successfully you need large, red, round tomatoes that are just a little too soft to be used in salad. It's a deliciously simple recipe from Umbria which can be served as an antipasto to accompany a roast, or as part of an all-vegetable meal with an eggplant dish, a pepper dish, and perhaps a zucchini or bean dish.

SERVES 4

*4 huge ripe round tomatoes or 8 smaller ones
salt and pepper
½ teaspoon tomato paste
1 cup soft white bread crumbs
a handful of fresh parsley, chopped
2 cloves garlic, finely chopped
3 tablespoons olive oil
2 large eggs, beaten
oil for greasing*

Wash the tomatoes and cut them in half horizontally. Scoop out the inside pulp with great care and sprinkle the inside of the tomatoes with salt. Turn them upside down on the draining board.

Mix the bread crumbs with plenty of salt, pepper, the tomato paste, parsley, garlic, oil, and eggs, then spoon this mixture into the tomatoes. Arrange them in a greased ovenproof dish and bake in a 400°F oven for about 15 minutes. Serve at once.

POMODORI A RAGANATI

BAKED TOMATOES

The cooking term "a raganati" comes from Apulia and means the same as "au gratin," when things are covered in bread crumbs and then baked in the oven until golden.

SERVES 4

4 large ripe beefsteak or Marmande tomatoes
a large handful of fresh parsley leaves
a small handful of fresh basil leaves
a very small handful of fresh mint leaves
4 tablespoons pecorino or Parmesan cheese, grated
¼ teaspoon tomato paste
4 tablespoons soft white bread crumbs
salt and pepper
olive oil

Wash the tomatoes and cut them in half horizontally. Wash and dry the herbs, chop them finely together, and mix with the grated cheese, tomato paste, and bread crumbs. Use more cheese than bread if the cheese is not very strongly flavored, less if it's very mature. Season to taste with salt and pepper.

Remove the seeds from the tomatoes. Arrange the 8 halves in an oiled ovenproof dish. Fill and coat each half with the mixture of herbs, bread crumbs, and cheese. Sprinkle with a little oil and bake in a 400°F oven for 15 minutes. Serve the grilled tomatoes cold, hot, or just room temperature.

PEPERONI IMBOTTITI

STUFFED PEPPERS

The success of this wonderful Campanian specialty depends upon the sweetness and juicy texture of bell peppers in the summertime. They must be red and yellow and carefully singed over a naked flame to remove all the outer transparent skin.

An alternative to this filling can be made with small pasta shapes boiled until soft, then tossed with olive oil, capers, chopped anchovies, and olives.

SERVES 4

4 juicy fat red and yellow bell peppers
3 tablespoons olive oil
4 slices of white, slightly stale bread
1 tablespoon anchovy fillets, drained and cut lengthwise
into thinner strips
1 tablespoon black olives, stoned and chopped
1 teaspoon capers, washed and chopped
1 large clove garlic, finely chopped
a pinch of dried oregano
salt and pepper

Spear each pepper onto a long-handled fork and hold them, one at a time, over a naked flame, turning the fork so that the pepper blisters all over and goes black. Rub off the outer skin carefully with your fingers, taking care not to split the flesh.

Cut off the end without the stalk and very carefully remove the seeds and membranes from inside the pepper.

Heat enough oil in a frying pan to almost deep fry the bread cubes and fry until golden. Remove with a slotted spoon and drain on paper towels. Mix the fried bread with the strips of anchovy, the olives, capers, garlic, oregano, and chopped pepper ends. Season well.

Spoon the filling into the peppers, then arrange them, upright, sitting on the stalk in an oiled ovenproof dish. Drizzle a little oil over them and warm them through in a 250°F oven to let the flavors blend for 15 minutes. Serve hot or cold.

(p 112) SPINACI ALLA ROMANO *left (p 108)* PANZANELLA
right (p 115)

PANZANELLA

BREAD AND TOMATO SALAD

This is a perfect dish for a summer holiday: it can be made in advance, requires no cooking, and is both filling and delicious. My mother can remember her childhood in Tuscany when the sea was so unpolluted that the bread was dipped in the sea, wrapped in a clean cloth, to soak it through. Sadly, this is inadvisable in this day and age.

SERVES 4

8 thick slices coarse country-style bread
5 large ripe firm tomatoes
1–2 seeded cucumbers
1 large onion
8 fresh basil leaves
6 tablespoons olive oil
2 tablespoons wine vinegar
salt and pepper

Cover the bread in cold water and leave it to soak for about 5 minutes. Squeeze the bread dry in your hands, then put it in a salad bowl.

Slice the tomatoes, cucumber, and onion finely, then mix into the bread. Tear the basil into tiny pieces and mix it in also. Dribble over the olive oil and vinegar (more olive oil and vinegar can be used if you like a richer dish), season with salt and plenty of pepper, and keep in a cool place until required — it is best if left for at least 2 hours.

MAPPINA

CHRISTMAS SALAD

This salad is a Calabrian specialty — part of the Christmas scene in the city of Cosenza. It's certainly very unusual, definitely not heavy, and the chili will aid your digestion.

BEAN-PICKING NEAR LIVORNO *In Tuscany the beans are ready for harvesting in July: some will be eaten fresh in salad and stews, the remainder dried and saved for the winter months to come.*

SERVES 8

2–3 heads of curly endive or escarole,
or a mixture of both
4 tablespoons olive oil
3 cloves garlic, chopped
1 mild, fresh chili and 2 small dried hot chilies,
seeded and chopped
salt

Wash and drain the leaves, dry very carefully, and chop coarsely. Mix the leaves in a wide bowl, sprinkle with olive oil, and sprinkle chopped garlic, chili and salt all over it. Put a plate on top and a weight on top of the plate. Leave in a cool place to rest for 2–3 days before eating it.

MELANZANE A MANNELLA

EGGPLANT SALAD

This is a wonderful antipasto, an eggplant salad flavored with garlic and vinegar. Success depends upon the frying — the eggplant must not be greasy.

SERVES 8

4 large eggplants
salt and pepper
oil for deep frying
3 tablespoons wine vinegar
3 cloves garlic, chopped
a large pinch of dried oregano

Slice the eggplants lengthwise and arrange them in a wide colander. Scatter over plenty of salt and put a plate on top. Place a heavy weight on the plate and leave them for 1 hour to drain out all their bitter juices.

Heat the oil in a deep-fat fryer or deep skillet to 385°F. Meanwhile, drain, wash, and dry the eggplant slices. Fry them quickly in the oil until crisp and golden, then drain on paper towels and cool.

When they are cold, arrange one layer in an ovenproof dish. Sprinkle over vinegar, oregano, and all the garlic and season well. Cover with more eggplant and this time add vinegar and oregano. Place a lid or aluminum foil on the dish and bake in a 350°F oven for 20 minutes. Serve cold, or at room temperature.

ZUCCA FRITTA

FRIED PUMPKIN

Pumpkin is very popular all over Lombardy, especially in the areas near Mantua which have been famous for their pumpkin dishes since the times of the Gonzaga court in the 16th century.

SERVES 4

1¼ lb pumpkin
milk
8 tablespoons butter
all-purpose flour
dry bread crumbs
2 large eggs, beaten

Remove all the seeds from the pumpkin and slice it thickly, removing the skin. Place the slices in a pan, cover with milk, bring to a boil and simmer until soft, but not breaking up. Drain and set aside to cool.

Put the butter in a large pan and begin to melt it slowly. Cover a flat plate with all-purpose flour, and another plate with bread crumbs and put the beaten eggs in shallow bowl. Dip the cold pumpkin in the flour on both sides, then into the beaten egg, then into the bread crumbs.

Fry in the hot butter over high heat until crisp and golden on both sides. Add more butter if required. Drain the fried pumpkin on paper towels, and serve piping hot.

FRITTO DI FIORI DI ZUCCA

FRIED ZUCCHINI FLOWERS

If you grow zucchini or marrows you know how many flowers you get in relation to the number of vegetables! This is a marvelous way of using up all these lovely flowers in a dish which is light and satisfying. Sometimes the flowers tend to be bitter, so it is always best to soak them in some lemon-flavored water for about 30 minutes, then drain and dry them very carefully.

SERVES 4

25 zucchini or marrow flowers with stalks and pistils
lemon juice
2 tablespoons all-purpose flour
⅓ cup cold milk
fine salt
1 large egg, separated
oil for deep frying

Soak the flowers in lemon-flavored water for 30 minutes, then gently shake out all the excess water and dry them very gently. Remove the stalks and pistils carefully and set the flowers aside on paper towels to finish drying.

Mix the flour into the milk and add a little salt. Beat the egg yolk into the flour and milk mixture. Beat the egg white until stiff, then fold it into the mixture.

Heat the oil in a deep-fat fryer or deep skillet to 385°F. Dip each flower into the batter, then fry in the oil until puffed and golden brown rolling them over with a slotted spoon. You should be able to fry in batches of 5 or 6. Drain on paper towels and sprinkle with salt. Serve hot.

PISELLI IN BARDINO *left (p 102)* ZUCCA FRITTA *right*

116

SEDANI CROGIOLATI

CELERY ROOT TOASTS

Celery root stewed in a deliciously smooth sauce, with generous amounts of butter, is served on slices of toasted country bread in this splendid dish from Piedmont. Turnip also works very well in this recipe, but celery root has such a lovely flavor and texture, it's best to use it provided everybody likes it. Try replacing a quarter of the stock with white wine and adding a couple of teaspoons of tomato paste. It's a dish worth repeating and would make a good opening course, or a vegetarian supper.

SERVES 4

3 smallish celery roots, about 12 oz each
1 small onion, very finely sliced
8 tablespoons butter
1 tablespoon all-purpose flour
2¼ cups stock
salt and pepper
4 thick slices country-style bread
chopped parsley

Peel and wash the celery roots, slice them into rounds, about ¼ inch thick. If using larger celery root, halve or quarter the rounds. Bring a large pan of water to a boil and add the sliced vegetable. Lower the heat and cook for about 20 minutes.

Meanwhile, sauté the onion in the butter until soft. Add the flour and mix it in, cooking it briefly. Add the stock and stir thoroughly.

As soon as the sauce begins to simmer and thicken, add the celery root and season with salt and plenty of pepper. Stir and simmer for 5 minutes. Toast-broil the bread in the oven (or toast it) and then arrange it on a platter. Pour the celery root and the sauce all over the toast and serve at once with a little parsley on top.

VINES IN PIEDMONT *The vines flourish in the pure air of this mountainous region of Italy.*

ZUCCHINE AL GUANCIALE

ZUCCHINI WITH BACON

This dish comes from the Marche region and is traditionally made with guanciale, a local specialty, made from the pig's cheek. It is cured in just the same way as pancetta, which is the usual substitute. It has plenty of lean meat inside the fat, so Canadian bacon could be used. The zucchini must be young, fresh, and tender for the best effect.

SERVES 4

12 small zucchini
salt
7 slices of pancetta or smoked bacon,
cut into strips
1 large onion, finely sliced
1 cup fresh parsley, chopped
2 cloves garlic, chopped
4 tablespoons olive oil
1 lb canned tomatoes, seeded and chopped
pepper

Scrape all the green off the zucchini and slice them lengthwise into strips the size of a small finger. Put them on a deep plate and cover with salt to draw out their juices. Leave for about 3 hours.

Sauté the bacon, onion, parsley, and garlic together in the oil until the onion is soft. Very ripe canned tomatoes don't contain many seeds. Just scoop out any you can see, while adding them and their juice to the pan. Give it a stir and continue to cook.

Wash and dry the zucchini and add to the pan. Stir and simmer for 20 minutes, then season with a little salt and plenty of pepper. Stir together before serving.

FRITTATA DI TARTUFI

UMBRIAN BLACK TRUFFLE FRITTATA

In Umbria the locals use the delectable black truffle rather like the rest of us use parsley — in generous quantities with not a lot of regard for its value on the market! In sizeable chunks, it flavors this rustic frittata to make it something really special. The important thing is that the truffles should be absolutely fresh and that they should not stew as the eggs cook, so make sure the frittata stays soft and slightly runny in the center. If truffles are out of the question, flavor the frittata with truffle paste to taste. A friend tried this for me with a small tube and suggested beating the eggs first and then stirring in the truffle paste so that it does not break up too much. This gives the frittata a more interesting color and texture, rather than an overall gray.

SERVES 2—4

4 oz black truffles
5 large eggs
salt and pepper
5 tablespoons light cream
2 tablespoons butter
juice of ½ a lemon

Brush the truffles, wipe them with warm water and a cloth and then grate or cut them into chunks. Beat the eggs with a little salt and pepper and the cream, then add the truffles.

Heat the butter in a heavy omelet pan until melted and hot but not sizzling or changing color. Pour in the egg and truffle mixture. Cook over low heat until golden on the other side. Then turn the omelet out on to a plate or lid, slide back into the pan the other way up. Cook until the other side is golden, bearing in mind that the center of the frittata should stay soft and runny. Cut it into little slices and sprinkle with lemon juice just before serving.

SARDINIAN CHEESES ON A BALCONY *Small-scale manufacture is what makes real Italian food so delicious — here eight rounds of fresh cheese ripen under the Sardinian sun.*

UOVA ALLA PIEMONTESE

EGGS COOKED IN THE PIEDMONT STYLE

The white truffle grows happily in the mountainous woods of Piedmont, where seeking them out is very big business indeed. Once there must have been a time when it was a simple natural food resource like berries and wild mushrooms. In the area around Alba, truffles are especially popular and many families spend happy hours with their

dogs seeking out the tubers for household use. They are always used simply. If you cannot find a fresh truffle, make the black truffle recipe instead.

SERVES 4

5 large eggs
1 white truffle
a handful of Parmesan cheese, freshly grated
salt and pepper
2 tablespoons butter
1 tablespoon olive oil

Beat the eggs, then thinly slice the truffle into the bowl using a truffle or cheese grater — it should almost be shaved! Add cheese and salt and pepper and beat again.

Heat the butter and oil in a heavy omelet pan until sizzling, then pour in the egg mixture. Cook the omelet until the underside is crisp and golden. Turn the egg and truffle mixture out onto a plate or lid. Slide it back into the pan the other way up and cook until golden on the other side, making sure that the center of the omelet stays slightly runny. Serve hot or cold.

FRITTATA
CON FIORI DI ZUCCA

FRITTATA WITH
ZUCCHINI FLOWERS

In peasant cooking, nothing is ever wasted and the flowers of the zucchini plant are deliciously sweet and tasty.

SERVES 4

about 12 zucchini flowers with stalks and pistils
lemon juice
all-purpose flour
olive oil
4 large eggs, beaten
salt and pepper

Soak the flowers in lemon-flavored water for 30 minutes, then gently shake out all the excess water and dry them very gently. Remove the stalks and pistils carefully and set the flowers aside on paper towels to finish drying. Dip the flowers in flour.

Pour enough oil into a heavy omelet pan to come to a depth of about $1\frac{1}{2}$ inches and heat until sizzling. Add the flowers in batches and fry until golden and crisp on all sides. Spoon out most of the oil and return all the flowers to the pan.

Season the beaten eggs, with salt and pepper, then pour them over all the flowers. Cook the frittata until the underside is golden. Turn it out on to a plate or lid. Slide it back into the pan the other way up and cook until the other side is golden.

FRITTATA AFFOGATA

DROWNED FRITTATA

This traditional specialty from the area around the beautiful city of Arezzo is a delicious alternative to a pasta dish. It consists of strips of firm frittata topped with a tomato sauce and cheese. Served with a crisp salad and plenty of bread to soak up the sauce, it makes a lovely supper or lunch dish.

SERVES 4

5 large eggs
1 teaspoon all-purpose flour
2 tablespoons dry bread crumbs
salt and pepper
olive oil
1 onion, finely chopped
1 stick celery, finely chopped
1 carrot, finely chopped
1 clove garlic, finely chopped
6 canned tomatoes, seeded and chopped

Beat the eggs in a bowl with the flour, bread crumbs and salt and pepper. Heat a little oil in a heavy omelet pan until sizzling, then pour in the egg mixture. Cook until crisp and golden, then turn it out onto a plate or lid and slide it back into the pan the other way up and cook until the underside is golden. Slide it out on to paper towels, drain, and leave to go completely cold.

Meanwhile, fry the onion, celery, and carrot in the omelet pan until the onion is soft, then add the garlic and tomatoes. Season with salt and pepper, mix well and simmer until you have a smooth rich sauce, about 20 minutes. Slice the omelet into strips, add to the tomato sauce and heat through for 5 minutes before serving.

In a heavy omelet pan, fry the bacon in the oil until crisp and all the fat has run out. Italians, like Americans, think perfect bacon consists of well-crisped fat, and not pink lean meat. Beat the eggs with salt and pepper, then pour on top of the bacon.

Cook the frittata over low heat until the underside is crisp and golden, then turn it out onto a plate or lid and slide it back into the pan the other way up and cook until the other side is golden. Serve at once.

US IN FONGHET

EGGS IN A
TOMATO AND MUSHROOM SAUCE

This is a specialty of the peasant cuisine of Venezia Giulia. It is generally considered not to be the sort of dish to serve to a special guest — which is a shame as the flavor is so delicious, especially when the wild mushroom season is at its peak in the fall.

SERVES 8

8 large eggs
salt and pepper
a handful of fresh parsley leaves, finely chopped
1 tablespoon olive oil
3 tablespoons butter
2 cloves garlic, chopped
8 oz fresh porcini (ceps), or other fresh
wild mushrooms, sliced
1 cup canned tomatoes, seeded, and chopped

Place the eggs in a pan of cold water, bring to a boil and cook for 6 minutes. Remove from the heat, dip in cold water and remove the shells. Cut them in half lengthwise, sprinkle with salt and pepper, and then with the parsley.

Sauté the oil, butter, and garlic together for a minute in a wide pan. Add the mushrooms and the tomatoes, stir, and cook for 10 minutes. Arrange the eggs, cut side up, in the sauce. Add a little water and cook over very low heat for a further 10 minutes, spooning the sauce over the eggs from time to time. Serve hot as a starter or with fried slices of polenta (page 54) as a main course.

BACKSTREET SHOP *The four vital provisions are sold at every corner shop — olive oil, grana cheese, prosciutto, and wine.*
CYPRESS TREE AVENUE *(p 128) The avenue of cypress trees this farmer has planted to divide his meadow from the plowed land, casts a beautiful striped shadow.*

FRITTATA CON GLI ZOCCOLI

BACON FRITTATA

This bacon omelet is a typical Tuscan country dish. It is perfection when accompanied by a radicchio salad.

SERVES 4

4 slices smoked bacon,
diced
5 tablespoons olive oil
5 large eggs
salt and pepper

MOZZARELLA IMPANATA

FRIED MOZZARELLA

Down in Campania they love mozzarella only slightly less than they love tomatoes and there are many recipes for using it in different ways. Traditionally the cheese is made from buffalo milk, from animals first introduced in the 16th century. But even in Italy this is becoming rarer. The egg-shaped mozzarella are packed in their own whey, to keep them moist, and are sold in sealed packs in two basic sizes. It is a much-loved cheese for cooking because of the way it binds ingredients together when it melts. In this recipe it makes a delicious melted filling inside a crisp, flavored crust.

SERVES 4

2 large eggs
salt and pepper
all-purpose flour
2 cups stale bread crumbs
a pinch of dried oregano
10 oz mozzarella cheese
oil for deep frying

Beat the eggs in a soup plate or shallow dish with a little salt. Spread out the flour and bread crumbs on separate plates. Salt and pepper the crumbs generously and sprinkle with oregano. Cut the mozzarella into slices ¾ inch thick.

Dip the mozzarella slices into the flour, then into the egg, then into the bread crumbs. Heat the oil in a deep-fat fryer or deep saucepan to 385°F. Deep fry about 4 slices at a time in a basket for 2–3 minutes, then remove and drain on paper towels. When they are all ready, serve at once.

SERVES 4

4 salted anchovies or 8 anchovy fillets in oil
8 slices thick white bread
7 tablespoons unsalted butter
3 canned tomatoes, seeded, and cut into strips
10 oz mozzarella cheese, sliced
salt and pepper
a pinch of dried oregano
oil for greasing

Wash the anchovies, descale them and cut them in half lengthways, then cut each length in half again to make 16 strips. Alternatively, blot anchovy fillets with paper towels and split them lengthwise.

Cut the bread slices in half and spread one side thickly with butter. Then place a piece of tomato, a piece of mozzarella cheese, and a piece of anchovy on each slice. Season with salt and pepper and a generous pinch of oregano.

Grease a baking sheet, place the bread slices on it and bake in a 350°F oven for 9 minutes before serving.

CROSTINI ALLA NAPOLETANA

NEAPOLITAN ANTIPASTO

To get the real flavor of this popular antipasto dish you will need to try and get hold of proper salted anchovies. If you can't find them, use the ones preserved in oil.

CROSTINI ALLA NAPOLETANA *(p 134)*

FOCACCIA ALLA CECCOBEPPE

VENETIAN COUNTRY CAKE

One of the most thrifty and delicious of all the country cakes, this uses up all the leftover pieces of stale bread from around the house. It tastes good, even in comparison to modern cakes, and is superb at breakfast time.

SERVES 12

about 2½ cups stale bread crumbs
(as fine as possible)
2 tablespoons butter
¼ cup golden raisins
⅓ cup finely chopped assorted candied fruit
8 large eggs, separated
1 cup sugar
grated peel of 1 lemon
a pinch of salt
½ teaspoon lemon juice
about 2 tablespoons confectioners' sugar

Sift the bread crumbs and measure out 2 cups. Put these bread crumbs into a bowl and set aside. Butter a 3-inch high springform pan (or ovenproof dish), add the remaining bread crumbs, turning the pan to coat the bottom and sides with crumbs. Discard any excess crumbs.

Cover the raisins in cold water and leave to soak for 15 minutes, then drain and dry them. Mix the candied fruit with the raisins. Put the 8 egg yolks and the sugar into a large mixing bowl and beat until pale yellow and foamy. Add the reserved bread crumbs a little at a time, mixing all the time. Stir in the candied fruit and raisins, then the lemon peel. Add a pinch of salt and stir very carefully.

Beat the egg whites with the lemon juice until stiff, then fold them into the bread crumb mixture very carefully. When smooth and evenly mixed, turn it into the prepared pan and bake in a 350°F oven for 45 minutes. Take it out of the oven and leave for 1 minute, then remove from the tin and sprinkle with the confectioners' sugar. Leave to cool on a serving platter.

BUDINO DI PATATE

POTATO PUDDING

A Friulan pudding of Slavic origin, this one is made with potatoes, golden raisins, butter, pine nuts and various spices. Surprisingly, it's light and lovely!

SERVES 4—6

¾ cup golden raisins
1 lb potatoes, washed but not peeled
½ cup unsalted butter, plus extra for greasing
½ cup light cream, plus extra for serving
a pinch of salt
1 tablespoon all-purpose flour
½ cup sugar
a pinch of ground cinnamon

a pinch of nutmeg, grated
3 eggs, separated
¼ cup pine nuts
1 tablespoon confectioners' sugar for dusting

Cover the raisins with cold water and set aside to plump up. Cover the potatoes with cold water and boil until soft. Peel them and mash in a pan. Add the butter, cream, salt, and flour and mix together over low heat. Add the sugar, spices, and egg yolks and mix very thoroughly, then pour the mixture into a bowl.

Beat the egg whites until stiff, then fold them into the mixture. Pat the golden raisins dry and carefully stir them into the mixture with the pine nuts. Butter an ovenproof dish large enough to take all the mixture. Pour it in carefully, then bake in a 350°F oven for 40 minutes. Dust with confectioners' sugar and serve hot with light cream. The texture is much lighter than you might expect.

FRITTELLE DI ZUCCA ALLA VENEZIANA

VENETIAN PUMPKIN FRITTERS

You can increase or decrease the ingredients as you require for this recipe, because pumpkins are usually quite large! The end result is a light and airy fritter with a lovely orange color and an unusual flavor. Fritters are a very popular Venetian dessert and are traditionally served around Carnival time in February.

MAKES 30

1 cup golden raisins
2 lb yellow pumpkin, peeled, seeded, and cubed
sugar
⅔ cup all-purpose flour, sifted twice
1 teaspoon baking powder, sifted
salt
grated peel of 1 lemon
oil for deep frying

Cover the raisins in cold water and leave to soak for 15 minutes; drain and dry. Put the pumpkin in a pan, cover with water, and cook until soft; about 20 minutes. Drain it, then wrap in a cloth and squeeze out all the excess water.

Put the pumpkin in a bowl and mash it with 2 tablespoons sugar, the flour, baking powder, a large pinch of salt, and the lemon peel. Stir in the raisins. Mix it all together very thoroughly, incorporating air to make it as light and airy as possible.

Heat the oil in a deep-fat fryer or skillet to 385°F, then add walnut-sized balls of the mixture and cook until crisp and golden brown. Remove with a slotted spoon and drain on paper towels. Sprinkle with granulated sugar and serve them as soon as the last batch has been fried. The slightly cloying taste of the pumpkin is balanced beautifully with a glass of ice cold, dry white wine.

DOVES *Three dazzlingly white doves sun themselves on a pantile roof.*

FRITTELLE

FRITTERS WITH GRAPPA

To make these fritters you need a pastry bag with a wide nozzle. The secret of success is plenty of fat to fry the fritters in. Excellent for an afternoon snack among friends.

MAKES ABOUT 20

2 cups all-purpose flour
¼ cup superfine sugar
a pinch of salt
½ cup dry white wine
5 tablespoons grappa or a liqueur
2 tablespoons unsalted butter, melted
2 egg yolks, beaten
3 egg whites
oil for deep frying
superfine sugar for dusting

Put the flour in a bowl with the sugar and salt, and stir in the white wine, grappa, melted butter and egg yolks, to make a batter. Heat the oil in a deep-fat fryer or skillet to 385°F, so that it is waiting ready.

Beat the egg whites until stiff and fold these into the batter. Twist the bottom of a pastry bag fitted with a wide nozzle (so that the batter doesn't pour straight through) and pour the batter into it.

Standing well back, in case the fat spits, squeeze small quantities of the batter into the sizzling fat — you are aiming for a squiggly shape rather like a coil of a rope, so move the pastry bag in a circular motion as you squeeze. Fry in batches of about 6 or 8. Scoop out the fritters as soon as they are crisp and brown, drain on paper towels, and sprinkle with the sugar. Serve hot.

SFINCIUNI DOLCI DI RISO

SWEET SICILIAN RICE FRITTERS

The origin of these rice fritters is to be found in Sicily's Arab heritage. Apparently, one of the culinary habits in those times was to fry certain foods which had previously been allowed to ferment. These were known as 'sfinci' from which the Sicilians have derived their name for all manner of fritters — with potatoes, pumpkins, ricotta cheese, and many other things. They are crisp and very crackly on the outside, with a soft inside rather like an orange rice pudding.

MAKES 18

1¾ cups milk
1½ cups cold water
1⅓ cups short-grain rice
grated peel of ½ large orange
a large pinch of ground cinnamon
4 tablespoons superfine sugar
⅓ cup all-purpose flour
¼ oz fresh yeast, diluted in a little warm water
oil for deep frying

Mix the milk and water together and bring to a boil. As soon as they reach the boiling point, add the rice and stir. Cook for about 15 minutes then leave to cool. When cold, stir in the orange peel, cinnamon, half the sugar, the flour, and the yeast. Mix together very thoroughly, then set aside in a warm place, covered with a cloth, to rise for 2 hours — it doesn't puff much.

Heat the oil in a deep-fat fryer or skillet to 385°F. Using a wooden spatula and a spoon, scoop out even-sized lumps of the dough on the spatula and scrape them carefully into the hot oil with the spoon.

Fry in batches of 6 at a time until golden brown, then scoop them out with a slotted spoon and drain on paper towels for a few seconds before tossing lightly in the remaining sugar (you may need a little more sugar). Serve hot with icy, dry white wine.

STONE-BUILT FARM *A low group of primitive buildings hugs the hillside against a sweeping panorama of receding hills.*

146

PANVINESCO

GRAPE JUICE AND SEMOLINA SWEETS

These shaped pieces of grape juice and semolina make a tasty snack. Very easy and cheap to make when you have grapes growing all around you, they are always popular with adults and children. Buying 2 quarts grape juice is quicker, but doesn't have the same appeal as using and crushing your own grapes. If you want to make the vino cotto in advance, it can be bottled and kept in the refrigerator until you are ready to use it. You need at least 8 lb of grapes.

MAKES ABOUT 20

about 1 cup plus 3 tablespoons fine semolina
colored sugared almonds or sprinkles, to decorate

VINO COTTO
4 large bunches sweet white grapes
4 large bunches sweet black grapes

First make the vino cotto. Squeeze the grapes with your hands or a mouli to extract all the juice, then filter it through muslin to obtain a clear liquid. Put it into a non-aluminum pan and boil it slowly for several hours, stirring often, until it is thick and stickily-runny like honey. Allow to cool and store in the refrigerator.

Boil the vino cotto and trickle the semolina into it like a fine rain, stirring constantly to prevent lumps. When it is completely thick and lump-free, pour it out onto a marble top which has been dampened with cold water and spread it out with a metal spatula to a $\frac{1}{2} - 1\frac{1}{4}$ inch thickness. Leave it to cool.

Cut it into different shapes with pastry cutters. Decorate with colored sugared almonds or sprinkles and serve immediately, allowing 2−3 shapes per person.

DOLCE DI PANE E MELE

BREAD AND APPLE PUDDING

From the far northern region of Alto Adige comes this delicious layered pudding of apples and bread, guaranteed to warm you on a cold day. In the summertime, use peaches or apricots instead.

SERVES 6–8

*10 small, stale and slightly hard white rolls,
sliced into thin rounds
¾ cup blanched almonds
1½–2¼ cups red wine, more if required
½ cup sugar
1 lb apples, peeled and sliced
or stoned, unpeeled peaches or apricots
2¾ cups golden raisins or currants
6 tablespoons unsalted butter
light cream for serving*

Prepare the bread and put it all into a bowl. Slice the almonds in half. Mix the sugar and 1½ cups of wine and pour over the bread. Butter an ovenproof dish large enough to take all the bread and the apples.

Put a layer of wine-soaked bread on the bottom of the dish, then cover it with a layer of apple slices and a few raisins or currants and almonds. Dot with butter, then cover with another layer of bread and fruit. Use all the ingredients in layers until you have used everything up. Make sure it is moist with plenty of wine – you can use more if you like. Dot the top generously with butter and bake in a 350°F oven for 30 minutes. Serve warm accompanied by cream.

GRAPE HARVESTING *These women are harvesting table grapes, which grow high up on the vine and must be handled with great care.*

PAN PEPATO

SPICY BREAD

This is a traditional harvest time cake prepared for many centuries by the Umbrian peasants when the crops were brought in. It is especially a part of the culinary scene in Spoleto and Foligno, but the tradition has spread over the border into parts of the Abruzzi and you may well find it both there and in Rome at Christmas time nowadays. The name is deceptive: it is not a bread, nor is it spicy – black pepper is the only one. Rather it's a rich flat biscuit, stuffed with nuts and chocolate, very similar to the famous Sienese panforte.

MAKES 8 ROLLS

*⅓ cup raisins
⅓ cup shelled walnuts
⅓ cup shelled almonds
⅓ cup shelled hazelnuts
⅓ cup assorted candied fruit, chopped
⅓ cup semisweet chocolate chips, chopped coarsely
a pinch of salt
a pinch of black ground pepper
4 tablespoons honey
3 tablespoons warm water
about ⅓ cup all-purpose flour, sifted
oil for greasing*

Cover the raisins in water and leave them to soak for 15 minutes, then drain and dry. Blanch the walnuts and the almonds in boiling water for 30 seconds, then rub off their skins. Chop them coarsely. Toast the hazelnuts in a hot oven for about 3 minutes and rub off their skins also. Chop and mix them with the other nuts.

Mix the candied fruit, raisins, and the chocolate into the nut mixture. Add a pinch of salt and a large pinch of pepper. Dilute half the honey with the water and mix it in.

Add just enough flour to make a dough that sticks together – use as little as possible. Knead carefully, then shape it into 8 rolls. Oil and flour a baking sheet, arrange the rolls on it, brush with honey and bake in a 400°F oven for about 12 minutes.

FARMHOUSE IN CHIANTI *(p 150) This farmstead stands amid extensive vineyards, cradled by the wooded hills of Chianti.*

BOMBOLONI

FLUFFY DOUGHNUTS

Mid-morning and about 6 p.m. are the times of the day when bagfuls of Bomboloni are consumed by groups of local teenagers in Tuscany. The air is filled with the sweet and irresistible scent of the doughnuts frying, and wherever you look outside the shops there are groups of young people with their small motorcycles, hanging about munching . . . I remember when it was Bomboloni day at home and we children were kept away from the spitting fat in the safety of the garden and would line up outside the kitchen window waiting to be handed the hot cakes.

MAKES ABOUT 18

4½ cups all-purpose flour plus extra
½ cup sugar
grated peel of 1 lemon
½ teaspoon salt
5 tablespoons slightly softened butter
1 oz fresh yeast
about 5 cups oil for deep frying

Put 3¾ cups flour onto the work surface, add two-thirds of the sugar, the lemon peel, and the salt. Shape it into a mound with your hands and plunge your fist through the center to make a hole right down the middle.

Cut the butter into smallish pieces and put them in the hole. Knead the dry ingredients with the butter for about 5 minutes, adding just enough warm water to combine the ingredients. Crumble the yeast into a cup and add enough warm water to make a runny, smooth paste. Add this to the dough and knead it for another 15 minutes or until the dough is completely elastic. Put it into a lightly floured bowl, cover it with a cloth, and leave to rise in a warm place for 2 hours.

Transfer the dough to a floured surface and knead it for a couple of turns before rolling it out lightly to a thickness of about ½ inch. Using an overturned glass or a pastry cutter, cut the dough into circles. Lay clean cloths on 2 large trays, sprinkle them with flour and place the circles on the cloth without touching one another. Reknead the

trimmings, roll, and cut into circles. Cover with a cloth and leave in a warm place for 1 hour.

Heat the oil to 350°F in a deep-fat fryer or a suitable saucepan that is deeper than it is wide — there must be plenty of oil so the frying doughnuts can move around freely. When the fat is hot, add the doughnuts: put the side of the doughnut which was touching the floured cloth into the fat first. Fry about 3 at a time, rolling them over until they are puffed, golden, and crisp on both sides.

Remove them with a slotted spoon and let them drain on paper towels, then roll them briefly in the remaining sugar. It is very important that you keep adjusting the heat so that the temperature of the fat is as constant and even as possible. Serve the doughnuts warm.

BUDINO DI AVENA

OAT PUDDING

This very simple but nourishing and comforting pudding comes from the cold northern region of Friuli. It is a pudding of Slavic origin and is perfect for children.

SERVES 6–8

1½ cups oatmeal
2¼ cups milk, or more
4 egg yolks
7 tablespoons sugar
2 tablespoons grappa or a liqueur
(optional)

Spread the oatmeal on a baking sheet and toast lightly in a 225°F oven for 20 minutes.

Boil the milk in a pan, sprinkle in the oatmeal, stirring continuously over low heat for 10 minutes. Press through a sieve or puree in a blender, adding a tablespoon or so of milk if needed, to make a thick cream. Return to the rinsed-out pan.

Beat the egg yolks until fluffy, add the sugar, and beat for another 5 minutes more. Add to the pan. Cook gently for about 7 minutes, stirring constantly until it has thickened.

Dampen a small mixing bowl with cold water (or if it's for adults the grappa or a liqueur) and pour in the mixture. Chill for about 4 hours, before turning out and serving.

GESMINUS

ORANGE BLOSSOM MERINGUES

This is an ancient Sardinian recipe handed down for many generations. They were baked briefly in a baker's oven after the bread was removed and then dried out in the sun for several days. Once these meringues were made with jasmine essence, but sadly this is now no longer available. They now make them with orange-flower water.

MAKES ABOUT 50

2 cups slivered almonds
oil for greasing
1⅔ cups confectioners' sugar, sifted twice
4 large egg whites, at room temperature
juice of 1 lemon
4 tablespoons orange-flower water

Line a baking sheet with wax paper and oil the paper. Toast the almonds in a hot oven for about 3 minutes until golden.

Beat the egg whites until stiff, then beat in the sugar to make a light dry meringue. (This is a long and tiring job, much eased by using an electric appliance!) Fold the almonds into the meringue mixture, then fold in the lemon juice and orange-flower water.

Spoon the mixture in mounds onto the baking sheet. Bake in a 350°F oven for 2–3 hours until dry. Cool on a rack and store airtight until required.

PERSICATA

SLICED PEACH SWEETMEAT

Reputedly of Persian origin, this is a lovely chewy preserve of peaches. Quinces or apples can be used.

SERVES 6–8

3 lb ripe peaches (preferably white fleshed)
5 cups granulated or preserving sugar plus sugar for sprinkling

Blanch the peaches in boiling water for 30 seconds, then peel and remove the pits. Place them in a muslin bag to drain for 12 hours. When they have drained, weigh again – for 2 lb of fruit you need 1½ lb (3 cups) sugar. Put the fruit and sugar in a non-aluminum pan and boil, stirring constantly, until it reaches the setting stage – try a little on a plate. This takes about 1½ hours.

Pour the mixture into a shallow dish and spread it out to a depth of no more than ½ – ¾ inch. Leave it to dry out for 7 days, preferably in a warm place, then turn it out onto a platter and sprinkle it with sugar. Cut into squares with a sharp knife and eat at once.

TARALLI

CALABRIAN SWEET COOKIES

These sweet cookies from Calabria contain the ever present Calabrian ingredient of honey. The longer they are left to rise, the bigger and fluffier in texture they become. They are excellent with tea or accompanying a dessert wine like Moscato, or served for breakfast.

MAKES ABOUT 14

3 cups plus 4 tablespoons white bread flour
¼ cup fresh yeast
2 large eggs, beaten
2 tablespoons olive oil
2½ tablespoons honey

Pour the flour onto your work surface and make a hole in the center with your fist. Dilute the yeast with ⅔ cup warm water and pour into the hole. Knead together as you would a bread dough.

Leave the dough in a warm place to rise for 1 hour, then add the eggs, oil, and honey and knead again. Shape the dough into about 14 figures-of-8 and arrange them, well apart, on an oiled baking sheet. Leave them in a warm place to rise for up to 4 hours.

Bake them in a 375°F oven for about 15 minutes. Cool and store.

GELATO DI COCOMERO

WATERMELON ICE

The Sicilians are the masters of the art of ice cream and sorbet making. It is a skill they have learned over the centuries and which originated during the Arab occupation. The original version of this dessert was a blancmange frozen solid. Traditionally, it celebrates the Festival of the Assumption in mid-August. Various other marvellously cooling sorbets made with jasmine flowers, lemons, and oranges are also prepared during the blazing summer months.

SERVES 6–8

1 watermelon, weighing about 10 lb
3 cups sugar
2 cups less 2⅓ tablespoons cornstarch, sifted
1 teaspoon vanilla extract
3⅓ oz semisweet chocolate
⅓ cup chopped candied fruit (preferably orange or pear)
⅓ cup pistachio nuts, chopped
ground cinnamon, to decorate

Cut the watermelon into slices, remove all the flesh and push it through a sieve into a pan. Mix the sugar and cornstarch into the watermelon, then bring to a boil and simmer for 5–6 minutes, stirring constantly. When it has thickened, add the vanilla extract.

Pour the mixture into a dampened mold and freeze until mushy enough to support the additions. Beat to break up the ice crystals, then fold in the chopped chocolate, candied fruit, and nuts. Freeze in 6–8 dampened molds, or one big mold. Turn out and decorate with a little cinnamon before serving.

CROSTATA DI MANDORLE

ALMOND TART

This is a delightfully simple and delicious almond tart with the filling sandwiched inside. Perfect for late-morning or for afternoon, its dry dense texture is designed to accompany drinks of some sort.

This is another sweet, with its sugar and almonds, that came from the Arabs. Indeed Italian desserts divide into those that are plain by modern standards, and ones that betray an Eastern influence and are very sugary.

SERVES 8–10

4 cups (1 lb) almonds, finely ground
1 cup superfine sugar
5⅓ cups all-purpose flour
grated peel ⅓ a lemon
3 large egg whites
5 large egg yolks
2 eggs
a pinch of ground cinnamon
a pinch of ground cloves
butter for greasing

Mix half the ground almonds, half the sugar, the flour, and lemon peel. Add the egg whites, kneading them in to make a rather stiff dough. In a separate bowl, mix together the remaining ground almonds, sugar, and the spices. Beat the egg yolks and whole eggs and add, then mix to a smooth creamy texture.

Grease a 10-inch tart pan with butter and roll out the dough to make 2 even-sized circles to fit the pan. Lay the first circle on the bottom of the pan and spread the filling on the top. Lay the second circle over it, pinch the edges tightly closed all around, then bake in a 350°F oven for 30–40 minutes. Serve cool.

GNOCCHI DOLCI DI NATALE

SWEET CHRISTMAS GNOCCHI

This is my own variation of the most ancient and traditional dish for an Umbrian Christmas. It calls for pasta to be cut into squares, boiled, then tossed with the walnut mixture and eaten cold. I don't like cold pasta at the best of times – especially not when it's sweet and chocolaty – but the walnut mixture is so good and easy to make that I decided to use it in this way instead. Serve with chilled Vin Santo wine as an unusual end to a Christmas feast.

SERVES 8 – 10

50 walnuts
⅔ cup sugar
1 tablespoon dry white bread crumbs
¼ cup semisweet chocolate chips
grated peel of ½ lemon
¼ cup sweet liqueur
a large pinch of ground cinnamon
about 4 tablespoons milk, if necessary
3 cups plus 4 tablespoons all-purpose flour
1 large egg
oil for deep frying
confectioners' sugar for dusting

Crack open the nuts, blanch them in boiling water, then peel. Put them in a food processor with the sugar, bread crumbs, chocolate, lemon rind, liqueur, and cinnamon. If the mixture is very stiff, thin with a little milk.

Mix together the flour, egg, and as much warm water as needed to make a smooth dough. Knead thoroughly for about 15 minutes.

Roll out the dough as thinly as possible: this is important and a pasta machine would help. Cut into 1¾ inch squares and brush round the edge with water. Place a little of the walnut filling in the center of each one, fold in half, and press closed tightly. Heat the oil in a deep-fat fryer or skillet, to 385°F. Add the pasta, about 4 at a time, rolling them over with a slotted spoon until they are crisp and golden brown. Drain on paper towels, and dust with confectioners' sugar. Serve hot or cold.

GNOCCHI DOLCI DI LATTE

SWEET MILKY DUMPLINGS

This is a delicately flavored and delicious dessert, which is nevertheless very substantial! It is a great comfort food for anybody but is particularly good for old people, convalescing invalids and children as it has a very slippery texture.

SERVES 4 – 6

2½ cups milk
3 egg yolks
4 tablespoons sugar
6 tablespoons cornstarch
2 large pinches of ground cinnamon
a pinch of salt
2 tablespoons Parmesan cheese, freshly grated
2 tablespoons butter, melted

Heat the milk to boiling point and reserve. Beat the egg yolks in an enameled or other flameproof nonaluminum saucepan with about half the sugar, the cornstarch, a pinch of cinnamon, and salt. Mix carefully together, adding the milk a little at a time. Stir this mixture into a smooth, thick cream over a very low heat.

When the cornstarch has thickened completely, pour the mixture out onto an ovenproof dish so that it is ½ inch deep.

Sprinkle the Parmesan cheese, a pinch of cinnamon and the remaining sugar over the top and drizzle with the melted butter. Bake in a 350°F oven for 10 minutes. Cool for another 10 minutes before cutting into cubes to serve.

WINDOW IN ASSISI *For much of the year, windows are left wide open so those busy indoors can enjoy fresh air and scent of flowers.*

INDEX

Note: Recipes and ingredients are generally indexed under their English titles. Illustrations are not indexed.

ACKNOWLEDGMENTS

The publisher thanks the following photographers and organizations for their kind permission to reproduce the photographs in this book:

1 Pierre Hussenot/Agence Top; 2 Monica Fiore/Fiorepress; 3 John G Ross/Landscape Only; 7−8 Anthony Blake Photo Library; 22 John G Ross/Landscape Only; 24−25 Brian Harris/Impact Photos; 27 Guy Bouchet; 30 Anthony Blake Photo Library; 32 Riccardo Villarose/Explorer; 241 Anthony Blake Photo Library; 42−43 Gary Rogers; 44−45 P. Curto/Marka; 47 Jacqueline Guillot/Agence Top; 50 Christian Errath/Explorer; 55 Anthony Blake Photo Library; 57 John G Ross/Robert Harding Picture Library; 63 A Faulkner-Taylor/Robert Harding Picture Library; 64 Bullaty/Lomeo/The Image Bank; 66 Serge Chirol; 72−73 Fuirepress; 74−75 Zefa Picture Library; 76 Guy Bouchet; 84−85 Fiore/Explorer' 86−87 Pierre Putelat/Agence Top; 90 Zefa Picture Library; 92−93 Will McBride/The Image Babk; 96 Zefa Picture Library; 103 Liba Taylor/Hutchison Library; 104 Guy Bouchet; 106−107 L Coccia/Marka; 108 Guy Bouchet; 109 John G Ross/Robert Harding Picture Library; 114 Alex Dufort/Impact Photos; 118−119 Marcella Pedone/The Image Bank; 125 Christine Tiberghien; 126−127 Marka; 128 Christine Fleurent/Agence Top; 129 Guy Bouchet; 133 Marka; 140 de Gex/Hutchison Library; 144 G Buntrock/Anthony Blake Photo Library; 146−147 Serge Chirol; 148 Donatello Brogioni/Grazia Neri; 150−151 Zefa Picture Library; 156 Zefa Picture Library.

Special photography by Linda Burgess: 18−19, 28−29, 35, 36−37, 48−49, 52−53, 58−59, 69, 78−79, 80−81, 88−89, 95, 98−99, 112−113, 117, 120−121, 130−131, 134, 136−137, 142−143, 152.

Thanks to

The Criterion Tile Shop
196 Wandsworth Bridge Rd
London SW6 2UF

Fired Earth Tiles
37−41 Battersea High St
London SW11 3JF

Judy & Tony
293 Westbourne Grove
London W11

Lunn Antiques
86 New Kings Rd
London SW6

Richard Dare
93 Regents Park Rd
London NW1

Ann Lingard
Rope Walk Antiques
Rye
Sussex

Stitches & Daughters
Blackheath Village
London SE3

Tobias & The Angel
68 White Hart Lane
Barnes
London SW13

The Dining Room Shop
62/64 White Hart Lane
Barnes
London SW13

The Gallery of Antique
Costume & Textiles
22 Church St
London NW8

The Conran Shop
Fulham Rd
London SW3

J K Hill
Handmade Pottery
151 Fulham Rd
London SW3